The Art of Tying the
Nymph

Skip Morris

Fly-Tying Illustrations by

Richard Bunse

PORTLAND

DEDICATION

I dedicate *The Art of Tying the Nymph* to whatever omnipotent force bestowed upon fly tiers their greatest gift: opposable thumbs.

ACKNOWLEDGEMENTS

To the fly tiers and others who generously shared their skill and knowledge:

For their detailed instructions for the tying of their patterns: Cal Bird, Craig Mathews, John Hazel, Hal Janssen, Ken Fujii, Darrel Martin, and Al Troth.

For sharing their insight and experience in fly tying, fly fishing, or both: Dave Hughes, Rick Hafele, Gordon Nash, John Smeraglio, and Jim Schollmeyer.

Finally, thanks to those who did such fine work with all the technical details and challenges that made *The Art of Tying the Nymph* possible: Brian Rose, Richard Bunse, Jim Schollmeyer, Tony Amato, Nick Amato, and Frank Amato.

Published in 1993 by Frank Amato Publications, P.O. Box 82112, Portland, Oregon 97282

Softbound ISBN: 1-878175-51-3
Hardbound ISBN: 1-878175-52-1

All photographs taken by author except where noted.

Front and Back Cover Photographs: Brian Rose

Book Design: Tony Amato

Printed in Hong Kong

10 9 8 7 6 5 4 3 2 1

CONTENTS

Scott Ripley Photo

FOREWORD

The dry fly may get all the glory, but for day-in-day-out ability to catch fish throughout the season, give me the nymph every time. After all, there are only a few times during the year when trout (and other species) have an opportunity to feed heavily upon the surface. The rest of the time they must forage underwater to find food, and this means nymphs and a handful of other creatures. Thus, the fly fisher who wants to consistently catch fish learns to tie and fish nymphs.

It wasn't long ago that nymph fishing involved attaching a glob of lead to your leader, tying on a heavily weighted fly, and trying to cast—or more correctly, lob—the whole mess into the water with some semblance of control. It wasn't a pleasant experience, and not surprisingly, it turned a lot of folks off to nymphing. Now, though, thanks to modern tackle, materials and techniques, all of that has changed. Fishing with nymphs is challenging, demanding and exciting, as well as an extremely effective method of catching fish.

But if you're going to catch fish on nymphs, you'll need the proper fly patterns, and the best way to have what you need, when you need it, is to tie it yourself. In this book Skip Morris takes the mystery out of tying nymphs, and he gives us a wide variety of both modern and classic patterns with which to fill our fly boxes.

Skip covers the entire spectrum of patterns that the serious nymphing angler will ever need: mayflies, caddis, stoneflies, lake flies, emergers, and tiny flies. He gives us both specific imitations and impressionistic ties. In addition, he discusses tools, materials, hooks, basic and essential tying techniques and more.

Skip is a master fly tier with more than thirty years of tying, teaching tying, and writing about it to his credit. He has developed many of his own nymph patterns and tying techniques, and he generously shares them with us in this book—much to our good fortune. Whether you are a novice or an advanced tier, you *will* learn something from this book. I know I did.

-Dave Engerbretson
Western Editor, *Fly Fisherman*
Moscow, Idaho
August 23, 1993

INTRODUCTION

Fly fishers today accept the artificial nymph as a valuable component of fly fishing, but this hasn't always been the case.

The nymph was once seldom used and low in status--to some it was sort of the fly fisher's version of live bait. Such thinking was particularly common in England around the end of the nineteenth and beginning of the twentieth centuries, and it is significant because England was the cradle of fly fishing and the home of many of its traditions.

This disdain for the artificial nymph made life harder for G.E.M. Skues, who really started the whole nymph-imitation idea into motion with his book *Minor Tactics of the Chalk Stream*. But Skues was the ideal champion for the nymph. His disposition and training gave him the ability to suffer insult stoically; to champion a cause steadfastly; to unflinchingly and repeatedly flaunt the truth, even when he and that truth were an itching, tormenting rash upon those around him--Skues was a lawyer. So as resentment against the artificial nymph grew, Skues continued defiantly to fish it, research it, and write about it. That Skues often and openly outfished the dry-fly purists of his trout-club failed to ease the situation.

I tell you of Skues to illustrate how low the nymph had sunk, in status that is. A chief criticism of the nymph was that it was too effective and therefore unsporting. From what I can tell, it was generally accepted back then that fly fishing was one of the *least* effective methods for catching trout, and therein lay its virtue. We now think quite the opposite--we consider the artificial fly the most natural, convincing trout-lure in existence. Today, fly fishers have to contend with hard-fished, previously caught-and-released, angler-conscious trout, and few of those fly fishers would avoid a fly or technique because it is too effective.

The artificial nymph has always had the advantage over the dry fly, because most of the time trout feed on real nymphs down beyond the dry fly's reach. But the artificial nymph has evolved to where it is now fished at every depth from the bottom to mid-depths to half-sunk at the surface to atop the surface alongside the dry fly (although fully floating nymphs raise some interesting debates on just what constitutes a nymph and just what constitutes a dry fly).

I tie flies, teach fly tying, write about fly tying, talk about fly tying for a living (along with a few other pursuits), and within these pages is most of what I know about tying nymphs. I contacted the originators of quite a few of the flies for tying information and samples, and those tiers were generous with specifics--all that they shared is here too. And that is still only a fraction of the knowledge and wisdom behind *The Art of Tying the Nymph*, because for years I have collected ideas and concepts and insights from far more keen and open tiers than I could now name. I am the author, true, but this book gathers its heart from all the collective passion of literally hundreds of fly tiers.

-Skip Morris, 1993

COMPONENTS OF THE NYMPH

Artificial Nymph

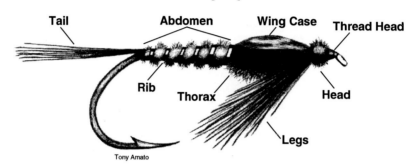

Tail   Abdomen   Wing Case   Thread Head

Rib   Thorax   Head

Legs

Tony Amato

Woolly Bugger

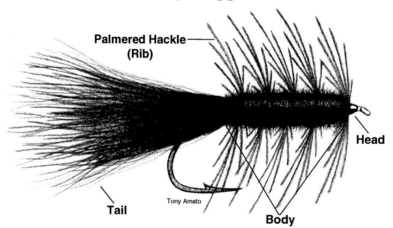

Palmered Hackle
(Rib)

Head

Tony Amato

Tail   Body

THE NYMPH DEFINED

To the "entomologist," one who studies insects, the term "nymph" refers to a specific underwater stage of aquatic insects. Artificial flies called nymphs clearly cover a much wider spectrum. The problem with a clear definition of the artificial nymph is that although fly tiers generally have a sense of what one is or isn't, that sense is hard to coordinate with nature. If, for example, an artificial nymph imitates all underwater immature insects prior to their hatching to winged stage, then the scud is out because it never leaves the water. And if we include all insects that live underwater, then we eliminate crayfish (crustaceans), leeches, and drowned insects that live exclusively on land, such as ants; and perhaps we *should* eliminate them, but many tiers wouldn't, and if we did, how would we then classify them?

If we look to fishing technique for answers, we find that nymphs may be fished with no imparted motion, a little, or a lot, and that artificial nymphs may be fished deep or right up in the surface film. No answers here.

And the question arises: Do we want to complicate everything with endless terms and categories?

Thankfully, a precise definition for the artificial nymph is a subject best reserved for fireside debates. The angler needs only the spirit of the word and enough clarity for communication—"They seem to be taking best on tiny nymphs today," or "I just started fishing deep nymphs this season, and it's sure productive." Such uses of the word "nymph" as these are easily understood. So I leave you with this shaky-but-practical definition: An artificial nymph is any fly that is fished sunk to suggest submerged insects and, with the exception of small fish, other fish-food creatures.

I
ESSENTIAL TECHNIQUES

"Essential" is the word—these techniques you will use constantly. They are listed alphabetically for quick reference. Tying instructions for specific flies will refer to these techniques as they are called for. Section IX, "Basic Techniques," describes other more-specialized techniques.

Adding Head Cement

All you need do is dip the tip of something pointed—a hat pin, bodkin, round toothpick—into a thin head cement and work the cement quickly around the fly's thread head. The thin cement will soak into the thread and dry rapidly, but you must watch that you add enough cement to secure the thread head without adding so much that it floods into and stiffens the fly's soft materials or fills the hook's eye.

Epoxy glue, my favorite head cement (see section X, "Nymph Tying Materials"), is fairly thick, so a tiny amount is added to the head and teased out into an even layer followed by more epoxy until the head is neatly covered. But for heaven's sake, keep the epoxy out of the hook's eye—epoxy is tough to remove. Flies freshly coated with any head cement can be stuck into wood or foam blocks until the coatings harden.

1. Coating a thread head with epoxy.

Dubbing

The word "dubbing" has two meanings to the fly tier: It is fur or synthetic fibers spun onto thread, and it is the action of adding fur or synthetic fibers to a fly. So tiers routinely use dubbing when dubbing their flies.

For right handers, cradle the bobbin in the palm of your left hand and clutch it lightly with your second, third, and fourth fingers; hold a ball of dubbing between your left-hand thumb and finger. There should be a few inches of bare thread between the fly and the tip of the bobbin's tube. Waxing the thread helps dubbing, but it's not required; another good approach is to rub the wax on your fingertip instead of on the thread. At any rate, now is the time to add wax if you so choose. With your right-hand thumb and first finger, draw a tiny amount of dubbing from the side of the dubbing ball; drawing the dubbing this way tends to align the fibers, which makes for the toughest dubbed flies. Use very little dubbing, as almost all beginning fly tiers use far too much. In fact, the best way is to start with almost no dubbing, and then add more until you have the right amount—which won't take much.

Hold the dubbing to the bare thread as close as you comfortably can to the hook; most of the fibers should be at a right angle to the thread. Spin the dubbing and thread between your right-hand thumb and first finger; spin in one direction only, otherwise you are spinning the dubbing on and then off.

Slide the dubbing up to the hook (or simply take a few extra thread turns later to start the dubbing onto the hook). Continue adding dubbing in this manner until all you need is on the thread, but cover no more than four inches of thread with dubbing—more than four inches requires too large an orbit with your bobbin which in turn makes for slow tying, so add more dubbing to the thread after the four inches is on the hook. Once the dubbing is on the thread, all that remains is to wrap it tightly up the shank.

A few pointers. Unlike most materials that are wrapped around a hook, dubbing can be neatly backed over itself to build diameter or fill in gaps. Tapered dubbed bodies can be created by adding the dubbing to the thread from almost none near the hook to thicker near the bobbin, or a tapered body can be created by building the dubbing layer by layer. For tiny flies, add dubbing to the thread in amounts so small that you can hardly see it—it will show up just fine once it is spun on.

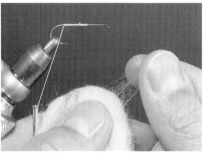

1. Hold a ball of dubbing in one hand and draw fibers from the ball's edge with your other hand.

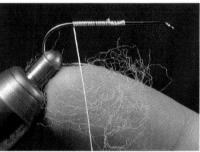

2. Hold the dubbing against the thread.

3. Spin the dubbing and thread between your thumb and finger in *one* direction.

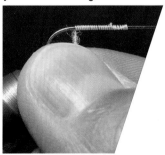

4. Slide the dubbing up the hook. Continue adding to the thread.

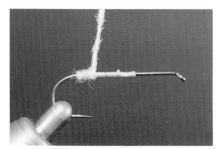

5. Wrap the dubbing-layered thread up the shank.

This is the basic method for dubbing; alternate methods are described in section IX, "Basic Techniques" under "Dubbing."

The Half Hitch

The half hitch is a simple fly tier's knot sometimes used in place of the more-involved whip finish to secure a thread head; three half hitches are usually used for this. When the half hitch becomes routine, it is time to tackle the whip finish. But there are other uses for the half hitch which, if you haven't already, you'll discover. Here is how it's performed (right-handers):

Begin with the thread coming from the rear of the head. Release enough thread so that there is about 7 inches between the bobbin and the hook. Hold the bobbin in your left hand and bring it up toward you until it is level with the hook; only light tension need be applied to the thread.

Extend the first and second fingers of your right hand and separate them about 1 inch. Bring the tips of your spread right-hand fingers down onto the thread; the palm of your right hand should be down. Now rotate and drop the wrist of your right hand until your right-hand's two fingers point up; as you do this, raise the bobbin, and then bring it down to the left until it is again level with the hook and the thread crosses itself in an "X."

At this point, the right-hand fingers should be pointing up and should be inside a loop of thread; the left hand, and the bobbin, should be to the left and level with the hook. In essence, you have already formed the half hitch; all that remains is to get it onto the fly's head and tightened.

Hook one side of the half-hitch loop over the fly's head. Hold the loop over the fly and then catch the loop with the first finger of the left hand; it easiest to catch the loop *between* the two right-hand fingers. Slip your right hand-fingers out of the loop; with your

right hand, pick up something to guide the loop as it closes: scissors, a needle, bodkin, or hat pin. Use this object to take the loop from the left-hand finger. Draw the bobbin down or toward you with your left hand as you guide the loop closed with the object in your right.

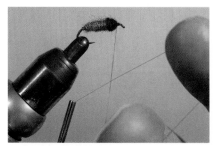

1. Create a half-hitch loop and hook it over the thread head.

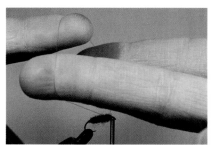

2. Pass the half-hitch loop to the first finger on your left hand.

3. Take the loop from the finger with a hat-pin, bodkin, or your scissors' closed tips.

4. Guide the loop closed.

Half hitch

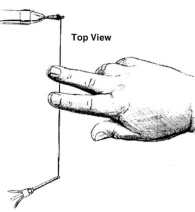

Top View

1. Raise the bobbin until the thread is horizontal. Spread your first and second fingers and bring them down until tips lie on thread.

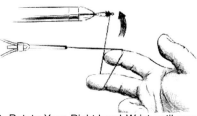

2. Rotate Your Right-hand Wrist until your fingers and palm point up; as you do this, raise the bobbin and then lower it to the left. The thread should cross over itself in an"X".

3. Hook the far side of the loop over the head.

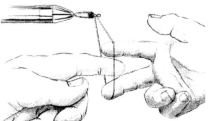

4. Let the bobbin hang. Take the loop from your right-hand fingers with the first finger of your left hand.

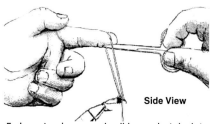

Side View

5. Insert scissors a bodkin, or hatpin into the loop with your right-hand and remove your left-hand finger.

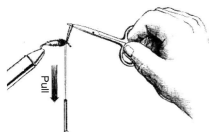

6. Pull on the bobbin as you guide the half-hitch loop closed.

The Light Turn

The light-tension thread turn, which I simply call the "light turn," is a handy, quicker alternative to the pinch for tying in stiffer materials such as wire and hackle stems. As an example, I'll describe how to use a light turn to tie in some oval gold tinsel.

Hold the tinsel near its end (oval tinsel is about as soft a material as you can comfortably tie in with a light turn). Hold the end of the tinsel along the shank at the tie-in point. If you hold the tinsel's end slightly towards your side of the shank, the thread's torque will draw the tinsel up on top of the shank. Bring the thread up and over the tinsel's end and down the far side, and then pull the thread tight. Add a few more tight turns of thread before proceeding.

The trick to making a good light turn is to use very light thread tension—just enough to control the thread but not so much that the material is forced to slide around ahead of the thread.

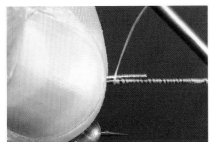

1. The light turn requires light thread tension.

The Pinch

The pinch is a technique used for tying in soft materials; it also offers excellent control. Here is how to execute it:

Hold the material between your left-hand thumb and first finger at the tie-in point on the hook's shank (right-hander's instructions). Bring your bobbin toward you and then straight up over the hook while maintaining

constant, firm thread tension. Move your left hand back slightly, but instead of sliding the thumb and finger back, *roll* their tips as you draw their joints closer together—this will widen the space at the front of the tips. Move the bobbin rearwards, towards the hook's bend, bringing the thread back between your thumb's tip and the material; keep bringing the thread back until it nestles securely in this spot.

With only slight tension on the thread, bring the bobbin back and down the far side of the hook as you guide the thread in between your fingertip and the material. You now have a loop of thread around the material. Move your left hand slightly forward and widen the space between your thumb and finger joints—your thumb tip and fingertip should now hold the material securely and enclose the loop of thread. Pull the thread tight, in turn closing the loop. Note that you have tied in a soft material while controlling its position on the hook.

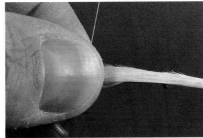

Performing the pinch.

The results of a well-executed pinch.

The Pinch

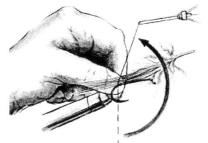

1. Hold the material to the shank. Raise the bobbin.

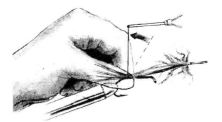

2. Bring the joints of your thumb and finger closer together; this will spread apart your thumbtip from your fingertip; slip the thread back between thumbtip and material.

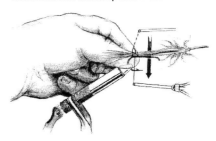

3. Bring the thread (and bobbin) down the far side of the material as you draw the thread back between fingertip and material.

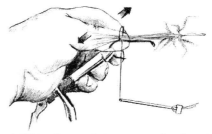

4. Widen the gap between your thumb and finger joint closing thumbtip and fingertip around the loop.

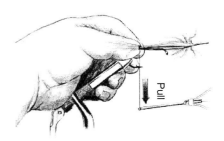

5. Pull down on the bobbin to tighten the pinch loop.

6. The material should be secured atop the hook.

Starting Thread

To start thread on a hook's shank, simply make four tight thread turns forward (toward the hook's eye), and then five or six tight turns back over the first four. Cut or break the thread's end and start tying.

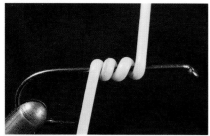

1. Make four thread turns forward (fly line is used for clarity).

2. Make six turns back to lock the thread onto the shank.

The Triangle

The "triangle" is my name for a method of forcing materials back from a hook's eye for ease in building a thread head. The name comes from the shape of the tiny opening formed when the thumb's tip and the tips of the first and second fingers are brought together.

To execute the triangle, simply slip this opening over the hook's eye and allow just enough slack to let the thread slip through. Then draw your thumb and fingers' tips back pulling hackle fibers, dubbing, or whatever material is near the eye back for clear tying access. On tiny flies you will be able to use only your thumb and one finger, but the motion is essentially the same.

1. The tiny triangle-shaped opening formed by the thumb and fingers' tips

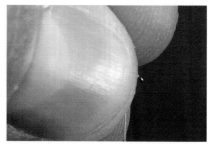

2. Draw the opening back over the eye.

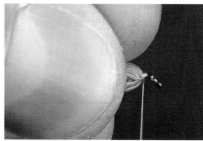

3. Draw back the thumb and fingers' tips, letting the thread slip past, and clearing the area behind the hook's eye.

The Thread Head

The thread head is merely thread wraps that cover material ends and build to a tapered shape. Sometimes, especially with heads that are large, steeply tapered, or both, it helps to add very tight thread turns near the eye, and then diminish the thread's tension as the thread travels up the head—the wraps at the eye form a solid foundation to keep the lighter turns from slipping (although all the wraps should be at least snug). Leaving plenty of space behind the eye helps avoid steep heads and the awkwardness of too little head space. The trend is towards tiny fly heads. I like a small head, but this is really a matter of style and personal preference.

1. Two thread heads: one is neat and tiny; the other is large but clean and gradually tapered.

The Whip Finish

The whip finish has intimidated more than one fly tier, which is a shame, because the whip finish is really only a half hitch that forgot to stop—it's easy. Look at it this way: The half hitch is a loop in which one of its sides is wrapped around the other; the whip finish is created when the side of the loop doing the wrapping adds more than one wrap.

Begin by adding a half hitch at the rear of the thread-head, but stop as soon as the half-hitch loop is hooked over the head. At this point, you have the side of the loop that is doing the wrapping, which we will call the "working" side, and the side of the loop which is being wrapped over, which we will call the "passive" side. The working side will be nearest you, and the passive side will be farthest from you. Grasp the working side in your left hand and hold it straight up under tension; then remove your right-hand fingers from the loop. As long as tension is maintained on the working side, it should keep the passive side firmly locked in place.

Now all you need to do is maintain tension on the working side as you pass it from hand to hand and wrap it towards the eye in three turns; as you do this, keep the passive side out in front of the fly—don't let the passive side slip behind the working side, or the turns you are adding will fail to enhance the whip finish's security. Close the whip-finish loop as you would a half-hitch loop, trim the thread, and add head cement.

1. Start the whip finish as you would a half-hitch; slip the loop over the thread head.

2. Lift up firmly on the working side of the loop and release the passive side.

3. Pass the working side from hand to hand as you add three turns over the passive side.

4. Close the loop as usual.

The Whip Finish

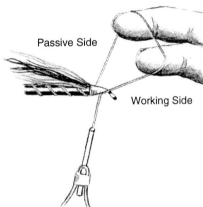

Passive Side

Working Side

1. Proceed as you would for a half hitch by slipping the loop over the head.

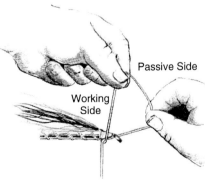

Passive Side

Working Side

2. Let the bobbin hang. Bring the passive side of the loop forward and keep it there as you wrap the working side forward in three turns.

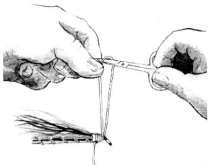

3. Insert scissors (or another pointed object) into the loop and take the loop from your left hand.

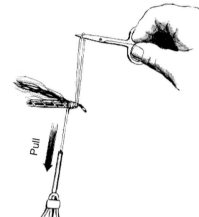

Pull

4. Pull the bobbin down as you guide the loop closed.

ESSENTIAL TECHNIQUES   11

II

MAYFLY NYMPHS

Introduction To Mayflies

Mayflies live most of their lives as nymphs, true nymphs, as opposed to larvae. Around mating time, the mayfly nymph forgets caution and swims boldly to the surface, struggles free of its shuck there, dries its freshly unfolded wings, takes flight, and at some point, mates. Swimming boldly and openly to the surface amid feeding trout may seem foolish but, in defense of the mayfly, plenty of God's creatures forget caution around mating time. The females return to the water to drop their eggs; often they die quickly after this and fall back to the water. There are varia-

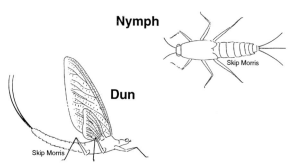

Nymph

Skip Morris

Dun

Skip Morris

tions on this, but in most cases it's accurate. The freshly hatched winged adult is called a "dun"; the returning egg-laying adult is called a "spinner." The nymph fisher is most concerned with the mayfly nymph, but the half nymph-half dun condition of the hatching mayfly is increasingly studied and imitated; more about this in section V, "Emergers."

Telling a mayfly from a wormlike caddis larva or pupa is easy, but stonefly nymphs and mayfly nymphs are similar. Also, mayfly nymphs vary considerably in appearance

from species to species, depending largely on their habitat. Perhaps the easiest way to identify a mayfly nymph is that it has only one visible set of wing pads which appear as a single hump that fly tiers call a "wingcase"; stonefly nymphs have two wing-case humps and a third, wingless hump. Also, most mayfly nymphs have three tails whereas all stonefly nymphs have two.

As I said, there is considerable variation in mayfly-nymph appearance. This is because mayfly nymphs move about in all kinds of habitats. Those that dwell in fast water are flat and broad headed; others may dwell in water from moderate to still, under rocks or buried in silt, and may be slim and delicate or stout and heavy-legged. Mayfly nymphs, like the duns they will become, can range from minuscule *Tricorythodes* imitated on size-twenty-two hooks to giant *Hexegenia* on size-four.

TYING DIFFICULTY
1 is easy; 5 is difficult

Fur Nymph	1
Gold Ribbed Hare's Ear	3
Skip Nymph	3
A P Beaver	3
Copper-Core Pheasant Tail	4

The Fur Nymph

Here is a mayfly nymph pared down to its most basic elements: a body and a tail. I ran across this pattern in John Juracek and Craig Mathews's book *Fly Patterns of Yellowstone*. Simple flies can be deadly, and this one has all the essentials of a productive nymph: tails, a nymph outline, and something (guard hairs in this case) to suggest legs.

The fur nymph is tied on a light-wire dry-fly hook because it is meant to be fished just under, in, or on the surface—the light hook helps keep it from sinking deep. The amount of floatant applied to fly and leader, or the lack of floatant, will determine if and how much the Fur Nymph will sink. It should be presented dead drift to rising or bulging trout during mayfly hatches. A nymph fished at the surface like this is dangerously close to being an "emerger," an insect that is in the process of escaping its nymphal shuck to become a winged adult—or, of course, an imitation of such an insect—more on this in section V, "Emergers." Juracek and Mathews especially like the Fur Nymph in dark brown and pale olive, but any color that matches the real nymph is fine.

FUR NYMPH

HOOK: Regular length, light wire, sizes 22 to 14 (the hook shown an Orvis 1523).
THREAD: 8/0 or 6/0 of a color to match the thorax.
TAIL: Three (to six) partridge-flank fibers.
ABDOMEN: Australian opossum, seal, or some other coarse dubbing (I sometimes use hare's mask), usually in dark brown or pale olive (other colors can be used).
THORAX: The same dubbing as that used for the abdomen, but added heavily, somewhat roughly.

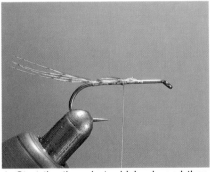

1. Start the thread at midshank, and then spiral it to the bend. Draw a few fibers from a partridge-flank feather to whatever angle to the stem squares the tips, and then strip the fibers free. Measure the fibers (they should extend a shank's length from their tie-in point), and then tie them in at the bend using the pinch.

   Raise the fibers' butts, advance the thread to midshank, lower the butts, secure them with thread turns using the pinch, and trim the butts (or just trim the butts as soon as they are secure under thread wraps at the bend). Work the thread back to the bend.

2. Wax a few inches of the thread if you wish (see "Wax" in section X, "Nymph Tying Materials"). Spin a tiny amount of the dubbing fur onto the thread; spin in one direction only. Wrap the fur-layered thread up the shank creating a tight, tapered abdomen to just past midshank. (For more on dubbing, see "Dubbing" in section I, "Essential Techniques.")

3. Dub slightly more heavily now, and perhaps more roughly too, until you've built up a thick thorax. But leave about 1/16" of bare shank behind the hook's eye for a thread head.

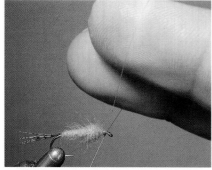 

4. Build up a small tapered thread head at the eye, add a triple whip finish, trim the thread closely. (For more on these steps, see "The Thread Head," and "The Whip Finish," in section I, "Essential Techniques.")

5. With something pointed—a scissor tip, a sharp toothpick, bodkin, or hatpin—tease out some fibers from the sides of the thorax; these fibers represent legs. Add head cement to the thread head (for more on head cement, see "Adding Head Cement," in section I, "Essential Techniques" and "Cements" in section XI, "Nymph Tying Tools."

The Gold Ribbed Hare's Ear and Weighting Most Nymphs

Here is the all-American nymph that nearly every fly fisher has tied or fished. Simple and scruffy, the "Hare's Ear," as most call it, is likely the most popular nymph in America. We will investigate how it can be tied best with unblended fur, and we will explore variations of adding lead weight.

Most often, the Gold Ribbed Hare's Ear is fished well down along stream beds, but it's a killing fly in lakes, fished well down or twitched ahead of rising trout.

GOLD RIBBED HARE'S EAR

HOOK: Heavy wire, regular length, 1x or 2x long, sizes 18 to 8 (the hook shown is a Gamakatsu F 15).
THREAD: Brown 8/0, 6/0, or, for the largest sizes, 3/0.
WEIGHT: Lead wire, size appropriate to hook size (optional).
TAIL: Guard hairs from a hare's mask.
RIB: Fine oval gold tinsel.
ABDOMEN: Hare's mask underfur.
WING CASE: Turkey quill.
THORAX: Hare's mask fur with lots of guard hairs.

1. Start the thread at about midshank and wrap it back to the bend. Wrap a short layer of lead from just behind midshank to about 1/8" behind the eye—but don't crowd the eye. This will create a fly of moderate weight. Wrap a few thread turns against the rear of the lead, spiral the thread steeply forward over the lead, add a few thread turns against the front of the lead, and spiral the thread back to the bend. From top to bottom: no weight, moderate weight, and heavy weight.

Snip a bit of fur from a hare's mask; cut close to the hide. Draw out the long guard hairs by their tips and set the underfur aside. Using the pinch, tie in the hairs as a tail. If some underfur remains in the guard hairs, no problem.

2. Using a light turn, tie in the oval gold tinsel just behind the lead. Raise the tinsel slightly, and spiral the thread down tinsel and shank to the bend. Snip off some more fur, draw out the guard hairs and set them aside, and add the leftover underfur to the underfur you saved from the tail. Spin the underfur onto the thread and dub a tapered abdomen to slightly past midshank.

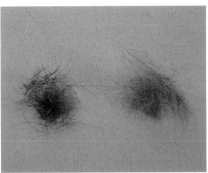

3. On the left are rabbit-mask guard hairs; on the right is the underfur that was pulled from those hairs. The difference is subtle, but the guard hairs are spiky, whereas the underfur is soft and fine—the difference is less subtle in the finished fly.

4. Wind the oval gold tinsel up the abdomen in four to six evenly spaced ribs. Secure the end of the tinsel under tight thread turns and trim the tinsel's end closely.

5. Wrap a section of brown mottled turkey quill, about one-half as wide as the shank's length, around the top half of the lead (or shank, if unweighted), and tie it in using the wing-case pinch. Trim the butts of the quill section.

6. Take up the set-aside guard hairs (which will still hold some underfur), and spin them heavily onto the thread. Dub a thick, rough thorax.

7. Pull the quill section flatly forward over the thorax. Secure the section with tight thread turns, trim the section, build a thread head, and add a whip finish.

8. Tease out some guard hairs from both sides of the thorax with a scissor tip, bodkin, hatpin, or the like. Add head cement to the thread head.

The Skip Nymph Dark and Substitution

The Skip Nymph, in both its standard and dark versions, is my own answer to the mayfly-nymph-imitation problem. I like that it is quick and easy to tie, that there is little tying in and cutting of materials, that its pheasant-tail-fiber back shows its subtle copper-wire rib clearly, and that its tails are soft and distinctly split. But I like most that day in-day out it convinces trout at least as well as any other mayfly nymph I have tried—and I've tried a lot.

The tying of the Skip Nymph is unconventional, but once you get the hang of it, it will go quickly. You can separate the hare's mask underfur from the guard hairs and use the underfur for the abdomen and the guard hairs for the thorax, as described in "The Gold Ribbed Hare's Ear and Weighting Most Nymphs," but this becomes less important for the Skip Nymph because its pheasant back smoothes out the profile. Since I first described the tying of the Skip Nymph in *Fly Tying Made Clear and Simple*, I have made a few small changes in how the Skip Nymph is tied; they make its tying easier and quicker yet.

When a fly tier says "substitution," he or she refers to the trading of one material or color of material for another. Usually, substitution happens when a tier doesn't have or can't get the material called for; sometimes the tier has the right material, but it is somehow deficient—too short, too dark, poor quality. But substitution can offer much more

than this; substitution can adjust or even improve a pattern. Adjusting a pattern might mean substituting natural gray duck quill in a pattern that calls for a wing case of pheasant-tail fibers, because the mayfly nymph being imitated has a wing case that is gray. Improving a pattern could mean substituting peacock herl for dubbing to give a nymph brilliance, to suggest some brilliant aspect of the natural.

Before substituting materials, there are a few questions the experienced tier will consider, at least unconsciously: Do I want to create the effect of the original pattern? Do I want to change the effect of the original pattern? What property, or properties, of the original pattern am I trying to preserve? What property, or properties, of the original pattern am I trying to change? Does this particular material offer what I want? Will I have to adjust my technique or approach in order to incorporate this new material?

Through the tying of the Skip Nymph, we will explore the principles of substitution.

The Skip Nymph may be tied unweighted, modestly weighted with copper wire as demonstrated, or more heavily weighted with lead wire. The Skip Nymph Dark is listed below; for the pattern of the standard Skip Nymph see section XIV, "Additional Nymphs." Fish the Skip Nymph as you would any mayfly nymph.

SKIP NYMPH DARK

HOOK: Heavy wire, standard length or 1X or 2X long, sizes 20 to 8 (the hook shown is a Dai-Riki 075).
THREAD: Brown or black 8/0 or 6/0 (or 3/0, especially for large hooks).
RIB and WEIGHT: Small copper wire.
ABDOMEN: Dyed-dark-brown hare's mask or squirrel fur.
BACK, TAILS, and WING CASE: Dyed-dark-brown pheasant-tail fibers, or dyed-black, or natural fibers dark-side-up.
THORAX: Dyed-dark-brown hare's mask or squirrel fur.

1. Start the thread at about midshank. Tie in an extra-long section of copper wire and wrap the thread down it to the bend. Dub a tapered abdomen to just past midshank.

Here would be a good place to substitute another dubbing fur, as there is no need for the spiky guard hairs of hare's mask fur. Muskrat, dyed or natural rabbit, squirrel, or even a blend of natural fur and antron fibers could be substituted either to save the hare's mask for the thorax or to create a new effect. A substitute for the copper wire could be used also—gold wire, silver wire, oval tinsel, even a heavy thread such as 3/0 or size-A rod-winding thread—but here, most substitutes will fail to double as weight under the thorax, a tying step we will soon cover, so this must be considered if you want a weighted nymph.

2. Draw a section of fibers to a right angle to the stem of a pheasant-tail feather; the right angle should even and square the tips of the fibers. The section of fibers should cover a length of the quill about equal to the full length of the hook. Hold the fibers by their tips and snip the fibers free close to the quill. Tie the fibers in, butts forward and tips back, atop the hook at the front of the abdomen. Tie in the fibers securely and work the thread forward up them 1/16"; then wind the thread back to the front of the abdomen. The tips of the fibers should extend beyond the bend a normal tail's length.

Suppose you have no pheasant-tail feather, what could you use? The fibers from another feather might work but, as you'll soon see, they will have to be tough enough to hold up as a wing case—when a wing case consists of fibers secured at each end of the thorax, it cannot give when a trout's teeth catch it, so it must be tough. The best substitute for pheasant fibers I have found is soft hair, in particular, squirrel tail. Squirrel-tail hairs make even finer tails than the pheasant, and squirrel is soft and lively. Some adjustments will be required later, but they are easy ones to make. Use red-fox squirrel for the Skip Nymph and dyed-black or dyed-brown or natural gray squirrel for the Skip Nymph Dark. You will find that it won't take much hair to do the job, and too much hair is awkward to handle.

3. Work the copper wire one turn into the dubbing. Draw back and down the pheasant fibers and secure them with a turn of wire. Tighten the wire a bit; and hold it stationary as you tug the pheasant tips out to the sides; the result should be a fan of tips. Now tighten the wire, but only firmly—maximum tension on the wire will weaken and even cut the fibers.

4. Continue spiraling the wire firmly to the front of the abdomen in five to eight ribs.

5. If you've read my first fly-tying book, *Fly Tying Made Clear and Simple*, you may notice that I've changed this next procedure since then. Draw back the butts and secure them projecting back with turns of *copper wire*. Add three (or two on a tiny hook, four on a large one) layers of copper wire over the thorax if you desire a moderately weighted nymph. Trim the wire's end. Work the thread to the front of the wire, add a few tight thread turns to keep the wire from spreading, and spiral the thread back over the wire to the front of the abdomen. For a heavy nymph you will need lead, which you might as well add as the first step.

6. Dub slightly heavily and roughly over the front of the hook to form a full thorax. Draw down the pheasant fibers' butts over the thorax and secure them just behind the eye. Trim the butts closely, build a thread head (slightly long, to secure the slippery pheasant), whip finish and trim the thread, add head cement.

If you substituted squirrel for pheasant, the squirrel's slipperiness will require some changes. Secure the squirrel tightly behind the eye with a collar of thread turns. Lift the butts and add some tight thread turns immediately in front of them on the shank to tip the butts upwards. Whip finish the thread *on the collar*, and trim the thread. Then trim the squirrel just ahead of the thread collar. This will leave a stub of hair butts over the eye. Because of this stub, a down eye is best with squirrel. You can also leave a stub if you use the original pheasant-tail fibers, especially if your wing cases sometimes slip from the thread head.

7. Tug two or three fibers out from each side of the bunch of tips, and then trim out the center—now you have created split tails. Tease some fibers out from both sides of the thorax with a scissor tip, bodkin, hatpin, or the like.

8. Here is a Skip Nymph tied with substitute materials: tan thread, dubbed muskrat-fur abdomen; gray-squirrel tail for tails, back, and wing case, and australian-opossum thorax.

The A.P. Beaver

The "A.P." stands for Andre Puyans, the creator of a whole series of nymphs commonly called the "A.P. Series." Within this series is just about every shade of mayfly nymph ever needed, and all are tied in the same essential form.

Fish any nymph of the A.P. series as you would any mayfly nymph.

A.P. BEAVER

HOOK: Heavy wire, 1X long, sizes 16 to 8 (the hook shown is a Partridge H1A).
THREAD: Black or gray 8/0 or 6/0.
WEIGHT: Lead wire (optional).
TAIL: Dark moose hair.
RIB: Copper wire.
ABDOMEN: Dark beaver.
WING CASE and LEGS: Dark moose hair.
THORAX: Dark beaver.
HEAD: Dark Beaver.

1. If you plan to add lead, add it now (for more on adding lead see "The Gold Ribbed Hare's Ear and Weighting Most Nymphs" and "Lead" in section IX, "Basic Techniques"). Comb, stack, and measure a small batch of moose hair for a tail. Use the pinch to tie in the moose at the bend. Take a single turn of thread *under* the hair tips to tilt them upwards.

2. Lift the hairs' butts, advance the thread to just past midshank, lower and tie in the butts using the pinch. Trim away some of the tail fibers leaving only four to six.

3. Use the light turn to tie in copper wire at midshank, and then spiral the thread down the shank and wire to the bend. Dub a tapered abdomen of beaver underfur to just past midshank. Wind the wire forward in four to six ribs. Secure the wire's end under thread, and trim the wire.

4. Pull the hairs' butts firmly back and dub the thorax. If you added lead, dub lightly; if not, dub heavily to create a full thorax. Pull the hairs' butts forward and secure them just behind the eye.

5. Draw four to six hair butts back along one side, and then secure them there with thread turns. Do the same on the other side.

6. Trim closely the remaining hair butts.

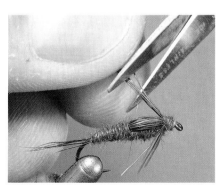

7. Dub over the cut butts with beaver underfur, build a thread head, add a whip finish, trim the thread. Draw one bunch of hair butts out to the side and trim them to length with a single snip. Do the same with the other bunch. Add head cement to the thread head.

The Copper-Core Pheasant Tail

Frank Sawyer developed the Pheasant Tail for his English chalk streams; it was tied with fine copper wire instead of thread. Al Troth developed the thread-bound Pheasant Tail most familiar to American fly fishers. When I was in a fly shop and saw some Troth Pheasant Tails tied entirely with copper wire—even a copper-wire head in place of a thread head—I realized that the blend of both patterns had a lot to offer. The Troth Pheasant Tail is the one I have always fished, and it is deadly, but weighting it was always a problem because the slippery peacock herl for the thorax tended to slide around on a bulging layer of lead. But fine copper wire can be built up for a smooth foundation, and since the heavy wire is spread throughout the fly, a great buildup at the thorax is unnecessary. I prefer to switch to thread for the final tying steps, but you can follow on through to the end with the wire if you like. *Do* remember to cut wire with old scissors or deep into the blades of a good pair.

When you wrap the fibers for the abdomen, you can keep them from escaping your grasp by taking a turn of them with one hand, pressing down atop the shank with a finger from the other hand to secure the fibers, and then reaching around with the first hand for the next turn. If the fibers splay, twist them.

Because a bobbin tends to kink and break the wire, it is best to work the wire in your fingers. But a bobbin won't be missed, since the stiffness and memory of the wire tends to hold its turns secure.

Al Troth once told me that he was experimenting with tying tiny nymphs with copper wire instead of thread because it is so difficult to get weight into flies smaller than size 18, and that illustrates another benefit of this approach. More on this in section VI, "Tiny Nymphs."

An unweighted Pheasant Tail can be tied in much the same manner as the copper-core version but, of course, with thread. I prefer to tie the unweighted Pheasant Tail in this manner: Tie in the tails; tie in wire; tie in more pheasant-tail fibers; wrap them forward and secure them with thread; tie in the wing-case fibers; tie in and wrap the herl (the herl is *not* spun around the thread); rib the copper wire up both the abdomen and thorax; from here, complete this Pheasant Tail as you would the copper-core version.

The Pheasant Tail is a fine match for dark mayfly nymphs. Fish it deep in streams, or just beneath the surface during a mayfly hatch. In lakes, fish the Pheasant Tail with a swimming motion from deep to just below the surface.

PHEASANT TAIL

HOOK: Heavy wire, regular-shank, 1x, or 2x long, sizes 20 to 10 (the hook shown is a Daiichi 1530).
THREAD: Brown 8/0 or 6/0 and fine copper wire (or just thread).
RIB: Fine copper wire.
TAIL: Pheasant-tail fibers.
ABDOMEN: Pheasant-tail fibers.
WING CASE AND LEGS: Pheasant-tail fibers.
THORAX: Peacock herl.

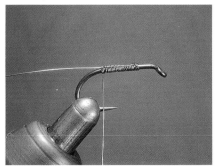

1. Start the wire about 1/8" behind the eye and wrap the wire back to the bend; hold the end of the wire *down* as you wrap back over it. Don't cut the end of the wire; leave it long.

2. Draw a section of about six to eight pheasant-tail fibers to a right angle to the stem—to square the tips—and snip off the fibers close to the stem. Measure the section and tie it in at the bend with one tight turn of wire.

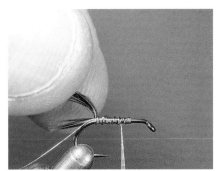

3. Draw the fibers' butts back and keep constant tension on the wire as you wrap it forward to slightly beyond midshank.

4. Wrap the fibers' butts forward to just past midshank and secure them with tight turns of wire.

5. Hold the tails in place as you wrap the end of the wire up the abdomen as a rib, secure the wire rib with the thread-wire and trim the end of the rib closely. Trim the pheasant-fibers' butts.

6. Square and snip another section of pheasant-tail fibers; this batch should contain about ten to twelve fibers. Measure the fibers to full hook length, and tie them in at the front of the abdomen. Wrap the wire forward a bit and trim the butts of the fibers. Now is the time to build some turns of wire for additional weight, if that's what you desire.

7. Start the thread at the end of the wire. Draw back the ends of both the wire and the thread and wrap the thread back to the front of the abdomen. Trim closely both the end of the wire and the end of the thread—now you are tying with thread.

Tie in two peacock herls about 1/2" up from their tips, and trim. Spin the herls and thread together and wrap both up the abdomen. Tie off the herls with tight thread turns and pull back the herls to break their ends (or just snip them).

8. Pull the fibers flatly forward over the thorax and tie them in about 1/16" behind the eye. Draw three to five fibers back along the near side of the hook and secure them with two thread turns. Do the same on the far side. (On small hooks, the legs may be omitted.)Trim closely any remaining fibers, build a thread head, add a triple whip finish, trim the thread, and add head cement as usual.

III

CADDISFLY NYMPHS

Introduction To Caddisflies

In truth, there are no live caddis nymphs; instead there are caddis larvas and pupas. No, actually there aren't even larvas—I checked several dictionaries and found that more than one pupa is "pupas" or "pupae," but more than one larva is only "larvae." "Larvae" sounded fine in a college lab, but it sounds pretentious to me anywhere else. Take the fly called the "Gill-Ribbed Larva"; if you wanted three of them would you ask for "Gill-Ribbed Larvae?" I don't like it, and I can't see why pupas should receive special treatment over larvas. But imitations of these larvae and pupae are called "nymphs" anyway, so as long as you're talking about artificials in general—"I'm fishing nymphs"—you'll avoid the larvae-pupas mess.

Caddis larvae live on the bottom of streams and lakes. Some larvae find protection in silt or under stones and sunken wood; others build protective cases and move about openly in relative safety, though that safety is definitely relative if a cased caddis wanders beyond the shallows—trout will eat case and all.

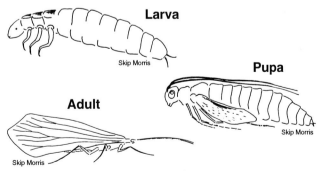

As hatch time draws near, a larva matures to a pupa. The pupa will come out of hiding and drift freely. Eventually the pupa begins its ascent. As it metamorphosed from a larva, the pupa built up buoyant gasses under its shuck. The pupa swims to the surface as its trapped gases are released to propel and speed the ascent. So it's a quick trip to the surface where the pupa hangs briefly and then emerges from its shuck as a winged adult. Though some sit atop the surface for a while, most caddisflies pop quickly from their shucks and take wing. Later, adult caddis mate, and then the females dip to the water to drop their eggs; some adult caddis actually dive and swim to the bottom to lay their eggs. Interestingly, caddis adults drink water—another draw to put insect within reach of trout. This is the usual scenario, but there are variations, such as those species that creep to shallow water to hatch rather then heading straight up, and those that hang at the surface for a long time or reach it and immediately pop through it to winged stage.

The nymph fisher, and tier, is concerned mainly with the larvae and pupae. But drown, spent adult caddis, and those that dive through the surface to lay their eggs, give new life to the old standard, largely forgotten wet fly.

Caddis larvae look almost like stubby worms with six stubby legs crowded onto their short thorax, except for cased caddis larvae, which look like the front quarter or so of any caddis larva with their hind parts hidden in a rough tubular case of sand or tiny stones or bits of wood. Caddis pupae look similar, but with a few alterations and additions: long legs, long antennas, and small well-defined wings along the sides.

Where to find caddis? Just about anywhere there are trout. Caddisflies live in still, slow, and fast water, and they are the toughest of the major trout-food insects when it comes to high water temperatures and pollution.

TYING DIFFICULTY
1 is easy; 5 is difficult

Rip Caddis	**3**
Deschutes Cased Caddis	**3**
Sparkle Pupa	**4**
Solomon's Caddis Pupa	**4**

The Rip Caddis

"What do you call it?" I asked.

"Rick's Raging Rhyacophila," he said.

"...Is that what you *want* to call it?"

I wondered at Rick Hafele's fly-naming talents as I inspected his caddis-larva imitation. It was simple: an abdomen of brilliant-green Krystal Flash, a short thorax of dubbed hare's mask. "The natural is really a bright green," said Rick. "It almost glows. I started with the brightest-green dubbing I could find, but Krystal Flash is the only thing I've found that's bright enough to do the job. Keep the fly; try it."

I did try it; it caught trout. So I decided to tie a few more. I took Rick's sample with me to a fly shop, but I couldn't match the Krystal Flash, even though the shop had a wide assortment of colors. The salesman said that they had carried that particular green, but that he hadn't seen it in a while. Back at my fly-tying table, I wondered how I could tone down the Krystal Flash (I had wanted to do that ever since I'd first seen Rick's fly) and, even when I couldn't find it in Krystal Flash, keep that particular shade of green. Besides, I wanted to find a method of tying the fly that would allow for the use of other kinds of reflective material—-everyone has a favorite, and new ones are always showing up.

What I eventually came up with combined Krystal Flash with the proper shade of dubbing, and some techniques I'd never seen before. Since the dubbing provided the color, the Krystal Flash needed only to add brilliance—I could add Krystal Flash, or any other reflective material, in almost any shade of green, or even clear, and get my subtle brightness in just the right color.

Rick inspected two samples of my new fly in his open palm. "These look good," he said. "Can you show me how you tied them?" We went to his fly-tying desk, hunted out the needed materials, and I showed him. "I've never seen that dubbing method before," he said.

"Neither have I," I said, "but it's still your fly, really. I just made a few changes."

"Let's call it the 'Rip Caddis'."

"'R' from 'Rick' and 'ip' from 'Skip'?"

"Right."

Well, it really *was* Rick's fly, so it seemed only right to leave it to his fly-naming talents.

Rick and I have since given the Rip Caddis its testing, especially on the Deschutes River, and for both of us it has been a consistent producer. Other colors can be substituted in the abdomen and thorax in order to imitate caddis larva other than *Rhyacophila*.

(When *The Art of Tying the Nymph* was about to go to press, I noticed a familiar-looking nymph in Judith Dunham's *The Art of the Trout Fly*. The nymph was Dave McNeese's, and I was amazed to see that its pattern called for "dubbing twisted with . . . olive Krystal Flash." Dave's nymph—the Green Caddis Larvae—is listed in section XIV, "Additional Nymphs.")

RIP CADDIS

HOOK: Heavy wire, 1X, 2X, or 3x long, sizes 16 to 10 (the hook shown is a Tiemco 3761).

THREAD: Brown small copper wire.

ABDOMEN: Three to five strands of clear or green Krystal Flash (or substitute) and small copper wire spun around light-green rabbit fur (rabbit of any caddis-color may be used).

THORAX: Hare's mask fur, dubbed.

1. Start some fine copper wire about two-thirds up the shank, as you would start thread. Trim the wire's end. Double three to five strands of Krystal Flash over the wire and slide them down to the shank. Hold the two halfs of the strands back as you wind the wire down them and the shank partway down the bend; use open spirals or, to add weight, close turns. (If you can hold the two ends of the strands separate as shown, it will make the next step faster.)

2. Put one end of the Krystal Flash strands in your material holder. Let the wire hang. Wax the other strands and add dubbing to them as you would add it to thread. (The more dubbing you add, the quieter the appearance of the Krystal Flash.)

3. Spin the wire and all the Krystal Flash together. Wrap this rope of wire, Krystal Flash, and dubbing up two-thirds of the shank.

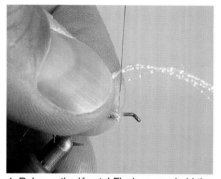

4. Release the Krystal Flash as you hold the wire taut. Tug the Krystal Flash free of the wire, near the hook.

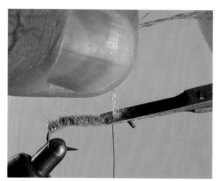

5. Secure the Krystal Flash with three turns of wire. Release the wire and trim the Krystal Flash.

6. Wax the wire again if you'd like. Spin hare's mask fur heavily onto the wire, and then dub to the eye. Half hitch or whip finish the wire, trim it, and add head cement. Tease out a few fibers from the sides of the thorax to suggest legs.

The Deschutes Cased Caddis

John Hazel, who teaches and guides on the Deschutes River all season long, developed this fly to imitate the great *Dicosmoecus* cased caddis larva, but other cased caddis can be imitated with it. Lots of anglers here in Oregon fish it—it works.

John has always formed the thorax of this fly with tightly wound dubbing; the idea is to create a segmented look. Once while I was tying a batch of Deschutes Cased Caddises, it struck me that the copper wire that secures the various case materials could be ribbed through the thorax to create segmentation. I gave the idea to John, and he liked it. So that is how you will see the fly tied here. John always weights the Deschutes Cased Caddis, so I will demonstrate its tying with lead, just as he would tie it.

Fish the Deschutes Cased Caddis well down in streams.

DESCHUTES CASED CADDIS

HOOK: Heavy wire, 3X or 4X long, sizes 8 and 6 (the hook shown is an Eagle Claw D58).
THREAD: Black 3/0.
WEIGHT: Lead wire.
RIB: Small copper wire.
CASE: Six strands of peacock herl.
HACKLE: Brown (or furnace,blue dun, grizzly), trimmed.
COLLAR (thorax): White rabbit fur, dubbed.
HEAD: Black goat fur.

1. Start the thread, add a layer of lead wire from about 1/8" ahead of the bend to about two-thirds up the shank, and secure the wire with tight thread turns. Using the light turn, tie in some copper wire at the bend; then use the pinch to tie six full peacock herls in by their butts at the bend.

2. Dub (any dubbing) over the lead to build it up a bit; also, use the dubbing to create a taper at the ends of the lead. Twist the herls together and wrap them up two-thirds of the shank. Secure them with thread and trim them.

3. Tie in a hackle (big, soft dry-fly hackles are good). Dub a short thorax up to just back from the eye. Palmer the hackle back to the bend.

4. At the bend, secure the hackle's tip with two turns of the copper wire; then rib the wire forward over the herl. The wire should be wrapped in the usual direction so that it will cross and reinforce the hackle stem with each turn. When the wire reaches the front of the body, continue ribbing through the thorax, but in close turns now, to create a segmented look. Secure the copper wire with thread at the front of the thorax and trim the wire.

5. Trim away the hackle's tip. Just back from the eye, dub a head of black goat. Create a small thread head, add a whip finish, trim the thread.

6. Pick some fibers out from the sides of the head, and then trim those fibers to leg-length. Trim the hackle fibers to a taper. Add head cement.

The Emergent Sparkle Pupa

With the help of scuba equipment, Gary LaFontaine studied caddisflies and trouts' response to them. This research brought fly fishers a number of new fly patterns, and the most widely accepted of these is probably the Sparkle Pupa. There are actually two forms of the Sparkle Pupa: the Emergent Sparkle Pupa and the Deep Sparkle Pupa. Here we will explore the Emergent Sparkle Pupa, but the Deep Sparkle Pupa is listed in section XIV, "Additional Nymphs." Both flies can be tied in a broad variety of color combinations—olive, gold, brown, yellow, white, green, orange—whatever suggests the natural. As with the Gray and Yellow Emergent Pupa listed, the veil color echoes the body color.

"Sparkle yarn," a yarn made of a synthetic fiber called "antron," gives the Sparkle Pupas their unique appearance.

This yarn creates an effect similar to that of the gasses built up under the real pupa's shuck. There is now a spooled antron which requires no combing; some tiers have switched to it, while others remain faithful to the original yarn for its wispy fine fibers. The method Gary uses to create the yarn bubble on his Sparkle Pupas produces just the right effect, but after tying a few hundred of them and experimenting, I worked out the method described here, as I find it to be quick and effective.

The Emergent Sparkle Pupa is usually fished dead drift, just under the surface; but an occasional twitch from a line mend, dropping the fly nearly on a trout's nose, and the Leisenring lift are all techniques that Gary describes as options.

GRAY AND YELLOW EMERGENT PUPA

HOOK: Standard dry fly, sizes 20 to 8 (the hook shown is a Mustad 94840).
THREAD: Gray 8/0 or 6/0.
VEIL: Yellow antron yarn.
BODY: Half-and-half gold antron dubbing and pale-yellow fur dubbing.
WING: Gray deer hair.
HEAD: Dark-gray fur dubbing.

1. Start the thread at midshank. Separate two sections from a length of four-section yarn. Comb the two sections with a fine-tooth comb. (Tiny hooks will require only a single section.) Tie in the combed yarn at midshank using the pinch. Trim the yarn's end.

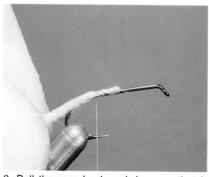

2. Pull the yarn back and down so that it slips around the shank. Hold the yarn under modest tension as you spiral the thread to the bend. The idea here is to distribute the fibers around the shank.

3. Dub a substantial body up two-thirds of the shank.

4. Cut the yarn so it is about two shanks in length. Hold the yarn back from the hook about one shank's length. Push the yarn straight at the rear of the shank to make the yarn fibers balloon out to the sides. You may have to try a couple of angles to get the fibers evenly distributed.

5. Push the balloon straight at the shank and keep pushing until your finger and thumb travel to just in front of the eye and the fibers are taut and distributed around the body.

6. Grasp the body, and the fibers, in the middle of the shank with the thumb and finger of your other hand. Slide your grasp again to just in front of the eye. Now the fibers are distributed evenly around the body and stroked to even tension.

7. Still holding the fibers, push your grasp back to the front of the body which will again make the yarn fibers balloon. Now the veil is formed; you need only secure it. This is the time to tug out a few fibers with a scissor point to suggest part of the shuck, although some tiers don't bother with it.

Work the bobbin and thread around the shank and yarn fibers under light tension, roll the thumb and finger back in a sort of pinch, and pull the thread tight. Working the bobbin for the turn of thread is awkward—you have to let it drop down the far side and then regrasp it—but it eventually gets efficient.

8. Add a few tight thread turns, and then trim the yarn. Comb and stack a bunch of deer hair. Use the reverse pinch to tie in the hair bunch atop the hook. Trim the hairs' butts and dub a short head over them. Complete the usual thread head. Trim the loose shuck fibers to about shank length, if there are any.

The Solomon's Caddis Pupa

Larry Solomon is well-known as an expert on the subject of caddisflies and fly fishing; his book *The Caddis and the Angler* covers this subject in depth.

The Solomon's Caddis Pupa is a detailed imitation of a caddis pupa, and it has its following. Though detailed, it is nevertheless tied with relative ease.

The Solomon's Caddis Pupa can be weighted or unweighted. It can be fished well down, dead drift, or allowed to sink and then worked slowly to the surface.

SOLOMON'S CADDIS PUPA

HOOK: Heavy wire 1x or 2x long, sizes 18 to 12 (the hook shown is an Orvis 1510).
THREAD: Dark 8/0 or 6/0
WEIGHT: Lead wire (optional).
RIB: Dark 3/0 tying thread (I usually use dark brown or, if the body is dark, black).
BODY: Dubbing, usually olive-green although any appropriate color may be used.
WINGS: Dark sections from the tip of a duck quill.
ANTENNAE AND LEGS: Brown partridge (hen saddle is a good substitute).
HEAD: Peacock or ostrich herl.

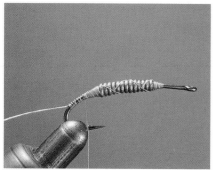

1. Start the thread at midshank. Using the pinch, secure a few inches of 3/0 thread; hold the thread under tension as you wrap the working thread down the shank and 3/0 to halfway down the bend. If you intend to add lead, do it now; the lead should run from the bend up two-thirds of the shank.

2. Dub from midbend up three-quarters of the shank, wind the 3/0 rib up the body (Larry prefers to wrap the rib in a direction opposite from the norm, but that's up to you), and secure its end with tight turns of the working thread. Trim the rib's end.

3. Snip a couple of sections from two matched duck quills. Tie in a section on each side of the body; the quills should be long-side down, and should reach down about two-thirds of the body. Trim the butts of the sections closely.

4. Using the pinch, tie in a six or seven partridge-feather fibers atop the hook sweeping back to the bend. Tie in more partridge fibers along the underside of the hook; these should reach to the hook's point. You can invert the hook for this if you like.

5. Tie in a single herl using the light turn, spin the thread and herl together, wrap the herl-thread forward to 1/16" behind the eye, build a thread head, and complete the fly as usual.

IV

STONEFLY NYMPHS

Introduction To Stoneflies

Like mayflies, stoneflies spend most of their lives as true nymphs. They clamber among the rocks in currents, usually swift currents; because of this need for moving water, stoneflies never live in lakes, only streams. I still sense wickedness when I turn over a rock and find a huge, dark, armored salmon-fly nymph clinging tightly to its underside. The slightly smaller brown-and-gold-mottled golden-stonefly nymph darts nervously and seems much friendlier. But in truth, the salmon fly grazes on plants; the golden stone is the predator, hunting and devouring the likes of caddis larvae and scurrying mayfly nymphs.

Unlike most mayflies or caddisflies, stonefly nymphs crawl to streamside and finally onto dry stones, brush, and trees to split their shucks and take wing. So there isn't a hatch, at least in the mayfly or caddisfly sense, but it is still called a stonefly hatch. Before the hatch—even a couple of months before—real stonefly nymphs are active and imitations are productive. But a stonefly-nymph imitation can be a good choice almost anytime in streams with substantial stonefly populations.

Despite the huge salmon-fly and golden-stone nymphs, stoneflies can be small, and small stoneflies can be important to both trout and angler.

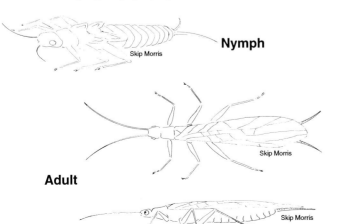

Nymph

Skip Morris

Skip Morris

Adult

Skip Morris

TYING DIFFICULTY
1 is easy; 5 is difficult

Box Canyon Stone	2
Brooks Stone	3
Morristones and Quiverstones	3
Early Brown Stone	4

The Box Canyon Stone and Weighting Big Nymphs

The Box Canyon Stone is certainly a standard salmon-fly-nymph imitation in the west. It is quick to tie, durable, and effective. The twisted-yarn abdomen is a clever way to create a segmented appearance.

Weighting a big nymph is a bit different from weighting most nymphs, partly because of the relationship between large hooks and lead-wire diameters, partly because wrap-pings of dubbing or peacock herl look slimmer on big hooks, and partly because the real nymphs that these flies imitate are usually corpulent, whereas smaller artificial nymphs often imitate slender mayfly nymphs and such.

Get the Box Canyon Stone well down in quick stonefly water. Mims Barker created the Box Canyon Stone.

BOX CANYON STONE

HOOK: Heavy wire, long-shank, sizes 10 to 4 (the hook shown is a Gamakatsu f-36).
THREAD: Black 3/0.
WEIGHT: Lead wire.
TAIL: Two dark-brown or black goose quills.
ABDOMEN: Black wool yarn.
WING CASE: Mottled brown turkey-quill section.
HACKLE: Furnace hen-hackle palmered over thorax (dark-brown and black are good substitutes).
THORAX: Black fur, dubbed (shown is rabbit).

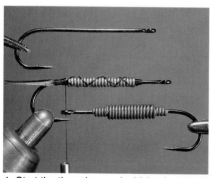

1. Start the thread around midshank, spiral it back to the bend, and use the pinch to tie in two goose quills as tails; the quills should curve away from one another. Weight the hook as you see fit. Here are examples of weighted big hooks; top to bottom: an unweighted hook, a moderately weighted hook, and a heavily weighted hook. See "Lead" in section IX, "Basic Techniques" for a discussion of using head color to indicate fly weight.

2. Use the light turn to tie in a length of wool yarn, and advance the thread to just past midshank. Twist the yarn tightly; twist it in the same direction it is naturally twisted. Wrap the twisted yarn up the shank and lead and, as you wrap it, twist the yarn more if needed. Secure the end of the yarn with tight thread turns and trim the yarn closely.

3. Using the wing-case version of the pinch, tie in a section of turkey quill. Trim the quill and bind the cut ends with thread.

4. Tie in a hackle by either its tip or butt, trim the hackle and bind the cut end with thread. Dub a full thorax.

5. Palmer the hackle up the thorax in three to five turns. Secure the hackle with tight thread turns and trim the hackle's end. (For more on palmering hackle, see "Palmering Hackle" in section IX, "Basic Techniques."

6. Part the hackle fibers atop the thorax and draw them down the sides of the thorax with your left hand as you pull the turkey section forward and down with your right (right-handed instructions). Release the fibers and secure the turkey wing case with tight thread turns. Trim the end of the turkey section. Complete the fly with a thread head, whip finish, and head cement.

The Brooks (or Montana) Stone

Charles Brooks wrote a number of books about western fly fishing for trout; the authority with which he wrote, the density of specific information within his books, and the ring of truth all tell of the formidable experience behind his words.

If not a true rebel, Brooks was at the very least unhampered by dogma or tradition. That his ideas still weave themselves through anglers' debates is testimony to that. One concept that is pure Brooks is that of tying nymphs "in the round." Brooks felt that artificial stonefly nymphs roll, whereas real ones don't, and that a nymph that looks the same from all sides will not appear to be rolling. Therefore the Montana Stone is tied in the round with no wing case and its hackles completely encircling its thorax.

I have seen the tying of the Montana Stone described by Brooks in several different books; each time, it is slightly different, and each time I am left with questions about the specifics of this fly's construction. The tying steps I present here are logical, and they are close to Brooks's own.

Because there is another popular stonefly imitation called the Montana Stone, many anglers have taken to calling Brooks's Stone the Brooks Stone.

BROOKS STONE

HOOK: Heavy wire, 4X-long, size 4 (the hook shown is a Partridge D4A).
THREAD: Black 3/0.
WEIGHT: Lead wire.
TAILS: Originally six fibers of black raven or crow primary split; I use dyed-black duck primary; some tiers use two goose biots.
RIB: Fine copper wire.
BODY: Black fuzzy yarn (wool yarn is shown).
GILLS: Gray or white ostrich herl.
HACKLE: One grizzly and one grizzly dyed-brown (or substitute standard brown) wound together, saddles or large, soft dry-fly hackles.
HEAD: Black fuzzy yarn.

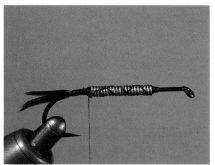

1. If you plan to add lead, wrap it from 1/8" ahead of the bend to 1/4" behind the eye and then secure it with thread wraps. Tie in a section of three primary fibers on one side of the bend and then another section on the other side.

2. Tie in the copper wire at the bend. Advance the thread up two-thirds of the shank, tie in the yarn—plenty of yarn—and then whip finish the thread and cut it. Trim the yarn's stub end.

3. Wrap the yarn forward a couple of turns, then back to the bend, then forward to its tie-in point two-thirds up the shank. Start the thread again leaving its end several inches long, and then secure the end of the yarn with tight thread turns—but don't cut the yarn or the tread's end.

4. Wrap the rib forward, secure it with thread turns, trim its end.

5. Tie in two ostrich herls by their butts where the thread's loose end projects. Strip one side of each of the two hackles and tie both in by their butts at the same spot. Trim both the herls' and hackles' butts.

6. Advance the thread. Wrap the yarn forward to slightly back from the eye, and then secure it with thread turns—no, you still can't cut the yarn. Wrap the hackles forward in about two turns and secure their ends with tight thread turns slightly back from the eye; trim the hackles' tips.

7. Spin the herls and thread together, and then wrap this herl-thread rope behind and against the hackles' stems to the hackles' tie-off point. Secure the herls and thread with tight thread turns; trim the herls and thread.

8. Advance the thread to about 1/16" behind the eye. Wrap the yarn forward, secure it with thread turns, and—finally—trim the yarn. Build a thread head and complete it as usual.

Morristones and Quiverstones

In *Fly Tying Made Clear and Simple*, I described the tying of my all-around stonefly-nymph imitation, the Morristone. As most stonefly nymphs share the same form and an overall dark appearance, the Morristone, in the appropriate size, has always produced for me. Here in the West, the stoneflies that usually capture the attention of both trout and anglers are the golden stonefly and the salmon fly. Both are big, corpulent, and often numerous. So, for those who fish most confidently with accurate imitations, there is the Morristone Golden and the Morristone Salmon.

Nymphs with rubber strands for legs are at times more effective than other imitations. When I came up with an easy way to add rubber legs to my stonefly nymphs, the result was the Quiverstone. The Quiverstone also has its golden-stone and salmon-fly versions. Rubber hackle, also called "rubber legs," has greatly improved in the last few years. Where once we had only thick, square rubber hackle, we now have it in a natural, rounded cross section in various thicknesses. I look forward to rubber hackle in a wide selection of natural colors, even finer thicknesses, and perhaps even with tapered tips. For now, what we have is a strong step in the right direction, and it's adequate.

Both the Morristone, with its hen-hackle tails and legs, and the Quiverstone, with its rubber tails and legs, are effective. There are surely times and conditions that dictate one or the other, but I have yet to figure them out.

In the smaller sizes, the Morristones and Quiverstones can get too thick with more than one layer of lead (although splitting the yarn from four strands to two can help); in the largest sizes, even with more than one layer of lead, an extra layer of yarn, or even two, may be needed to create adequate thickness. The contrasting belly may be omitted—often I do omit it—but if you are going for accuracy, or you think that trout respond to the belly color, it is worth the extra tying seconds. There are many materials that make good ribbing for the Morristones and Quiverstones—flat monofilament, Larva Lace, Swannundaze, even size-A rod-winding thread. If you have trouble getting the rib to start up the yarn body, take one wrap of yarn *behind* the rib material, and then wrap all subsequent turns ahead of the rib; this way when you wind the rib it is already started into the yarn body. Actually, if you omit the belly, you also have the option of omitting the rib. It boils down to this: How picky are the trout? and how picky are you? Try chenille or vernille in place of yarn on a Morristone or Quiverstone sometime; you may prefer the effect. Another material that shows promise for these nymphs is the new pre-dubbed thread, if it is thick enough. Some hen-saddle feathers are so full that the effect of legs is lost to two flat, brown wings. To cure this, take four quick snips from the hen after it has been pulled forward and secured, before the wing case is formed. The snips will leave four slots and six well-defined legs.

Fish the Morristones and Quiverstones as you would any stonefly nymph.

MORRISTONE

HOOK: Heavy wire, 3X to 6X long, sizes 10 to 6.
THREAD: Brown 3/0.
WEIGHT: Lead wire.
BELLY: None.
TAIL: Brown mottled hen-saddle-hackle tip.
RIB: Brown V rib.
BODY: Dark-gray yarn (usually wool or antron); chenille or
    vernille is a good substitute.
WING CASE: Pheasant-tail fibers, dark side showing.
LEGS: Brown-mottled hen-saddle hackle.
HEAD: Dark-brown dubbing (dyed rabbit is good).

QUIVERSTONE
    The same as the Morristone, but use fine brown (or black) rubber strands for the tails, and use medium-diameter brown (or black) rubber strands for the legs.

MORRISTONE GOLDEN

HOOK: Heavy wire, 3X to 4X long, sizes 8 to 4 (hooks up to
    6X long can be used, but the sizes must be correspond-
    ingly smaller).(The hook shown is a Daiichi 2220).
THREAD: Brown 3/0.
WEIGHT: Lead wire.
TAIL: Mottled brown hen-saddle-hackle tip.
BELLY: Rabbit fur dyed gold.
RIB: Small copper wire.
BODY: Dark-brown wool yarn.
WING CASE: Pheasant-tail fibers, light side showing.
LEGS: Mottled-brown hen-saddle hackle.
HEAD: Dark-brown dubbing (dyed rabbit is good).

QUIVERSTONE GOLDEN
    The same as the Morristone Golden, but use fine brown (or black, if fine brown is unavailable) rubber strands for the tails, and use medium-diameter brown rubber strands for the legs.

MORRISTONE SALMON

HOOK: Heavy wire, 3X to 4X long, sizes 8 to 2 (hooks up to
    6X long can be used, but the size must be correspond-
    ingly smaller).
THREAD: Chocolate-brown or black 3/0.
WEIGHT: Lead wire.
TAIL: Chocolate-brown or black hen-saddle-hackle tip.
BELLY: Tan (or gray and tan blended) rabbit fur.
RIB: Dark-brown V rib.
BODY: Black wool yarn (I'd prefer chocolate- or blackish-
    brown, but I can't find it).
WING CASE: Very dark natural or black-dyed pheasant-tail
    fibers.
LEGS: Chocolate-brown or black hen hackle.
HEAD: Black or very dark-brown fur (dyed rabbit is good).

QUIVERSTONE SALMON
    The same as the Morristone Salmon, but use fine brown (or black) rubber hackle for the tails, and use medium-diameter brown (or black) rubber hackle for the legs.

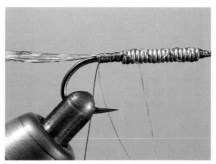

1. Shown here is the Morristone Golden, but the steps are the same for all the Morristones. Wrap lead from 1/8" ahead of the bend to 3/16" behind the eye, and secure it with thread. (A second, short layer of lead from midshank to about 1/8" short of the end of the first layer helps fill out the thorax; this can also be done with a short, spread layer of yarn over the lead if the extra weight is not desired.)

Trim out the tip of a hen-saddle hackle, snip the fibers close along the sides of the tip's base for about 1/8", and tie in the feather at the bend, curve up. Save the body of the hackle from which the tip came.

2. Pull some extra thread off the spool, double it over and secure it at the bend with thread wraps. The result should be a secured loop of thread; the loop should be beneath the shank slightly to the far side of the hook. (The loop and all the directions for the belly are omitted for the Morristone; a belly is only used on the golden and salmon versions.)

3. Tie in the copper wire, then the yarn. Advance the thread to just past midshank. Tie in a section of pheasant-tail fibers by their butts (the fibers should be light side down so that the light side will be up later). Tie in a second section of fibers over the first.

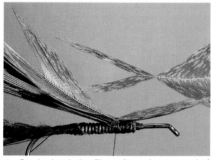

4. Stroke back the fibers from the *cut* end of the hen hackle; all that should project forward is about 1/8" of stem and its fibers. Tie in the hackle by this 1/8", curve up, atop the pheasant fibers. Trim the fibers' tips.

5. Advance the thread to about 3/16" behind the eye. Draw the pheasant fibers and the hen hackle forward, and then take one or two loose thread turns over them—these turns are temporary. Wrap the yarn up the rear of the pheasant fibers. Back off the loose thread turns to release the pheasant and hen. Continue wrapping the yarn to 3/16" behind the hook's eye. Secure the yarn's end with thread turns and trim the yarn closely.

6. Dub the belly fur onto the thread loop, slide the dubbing to the body, and pull the dubbed loop forward under the shank. Secure the end of the loop under thread, and then trim the dubbed loop's end. If you keep the belly fur slightly to the far side, thread torque will shift it into place. Draw the pheasant and hen forward and again take one or two loose thread turns over them.

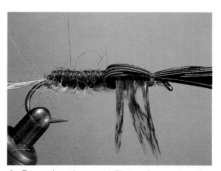

7. Wrap the copper wire forward in six to eight turns to the rear of the pheasant. Back off the thread to release the pheasant and hen, and then wrap the copper wire over the thorax in three turns. Secure the copper wire with thread, and then trim the wire's end closely.

8. Draw the hen hackle flatly down atop the thorax, and then secure the hackle with tight thread turns. Trim the end of the hackle.

9. Draw the pheasant fibers down atop the hen and secure them with plenty of thread turns. Trim the butts of the pheasant, and bind them with thread. Dub a modest head over the thread-bound butts. Build and complete a thread head. Draw two to four fibers out from each side of the hen tip, and then snip out the center, leaving split tails (See caption 10).

10. You have the option of snipping four slots in the hen feather to help define the legs. This is done *after* the hen is pulled forward and secured, and *before* the wing case is formed. (between steps 8 and 9)

13. Draw the rubber hackle back and take a turn of yarn tightly up against the previous turn. Wrap the yarn forward; then secure and trim it at the usual point. Dub, draw forward, and secure the dubbed-thread belly, if you desire it. Wind the rib forward as usual, but work it through the thorax without pushing the rubber strands out of position. While wrapping the rib, you can temporarily secure the pheasant fibers and rubber strands out of your way with a couple of thread turns, as you did for the Morristone.

From this point, complete the Quiverstone as you would the Morristone.

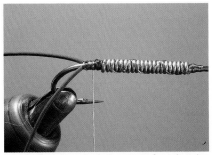

11. Let's take a look the steps for tying the Morristone that must be changed in order to create the Quiverstone. Before or after the lead is added, secure a length of fine rubber hackle on one side of the shank at the bend. Pull the end of the rubber hackle back along the other side of the shank and secure it there with thread turns. Trim these tails to length now or when you later trim the legs.

12. Continue just as you did for the Morristone but do not tie in a hen-hackle section over the pheasant-tail fibers. Snip two short sections of medium-thick rubber strand, and then set the sections aside. Wrap the yarn as usual to one turn ahead of the pheasant fibers (or two turns ahead for especially large hooks). Loop one of the set-aside rubber-strand sections over the yarn, hold the loop's ends in one hand, and then wrap the yarn as you slide the strand-loop into place on the near side of the hook. Before wrapping further, loop the other rubber section over the yarn, slide the rubber strand into place on the far side of the hook, and complete the single turn of yarn that secures both rubber-strand sections. The yarn should be taut and firmly back against the previous turn of yarn.

The Early Brown Stone

Most anglers think of the West when they think of stone-flies—broad, crashing rivers bursting with huge insects, insects that struggle to take wing, to raise their bulging bodies beyond the reach of the slashing teeth of great rainbow trout. The nymph fisher's version of this reverie is huge stonefly nymphs plucked from cover by heaving currents and snapped up by great rainbows or scraped from the river's stone bed by trouts' fine, sharp teeth. Very poetic, and not entirely unrealistic, but hardly common. Dry fly or nymph: either way the delux image is western stoneflies, western trout, western rivers.

But stoneflies can excite eastern trout as well, and when trout season opens on most eastern streams, it is a good bet that the early brown stones will be active and the trout will be onto them. Often at this time the early brown stone is the only insect of any kind to really interest trout.

The Early Brown Stone (sometimes called the Early Brown Stonefly Nymph) is a proven, popular imitation of its namesake.

This pattern seems to have a lot of versions; the one listed here is a fine one. Fish it dead drift, especially along stream edges where the naturals concentrate.

EARLY BROWN STONE

HOOK: Heavy wire, 2x or 3x long, sizes 14 to 10 (the hook
   shown is a Dai-Riki 730).
THREAD: Tan 8/0 or 6/0.
WEIGHT: Lead wire (optional).
TAILS: Dyed-tan turkey or goose biots.
ABDOMEN: Medium-brown fur.
WING CASES: Dark-brown mottled turkey-quill section.
THORAX: Medium-brown fur.
LEGS: Brown hen-hackle (neck or saddle, but I prefer
   saddle).

1. Weight the hook if you wish, but leave some bare shank near the bend. Using the pinch, tie in two biots, short, at the bend; the biots should curve away from one another.

2. Dub a full tapered   abdomen about two-thirds up the shank.

3. Just behind the eye, tie in a bunch of hen-hackle fibers; these fibers should extend off the eye a distance of about two-thirds the length of the hook's shank.

4. At the front of the abdomen, tie in a section of turkey quill. Cover the thread wraps over the section with dubbing, but leave plenty of room for another wing case and a thread head.

5. Fold the section back over a bodkin, needle, or hatpin, and then tie in the folded section at the front of the dubbing (the reverse pinch can be helpful here).

6. Fold the section back and bind it with thread wraps; the section should now project back. Dub again.

7. Draw about half the hen-hackle fibers back along one side of the thorax and bind them there with a few thread turns. Do the same with the remaining fibers on the other side.

8. Fold the quill section again, bind it, trim it closely, build and complete the usual thread head.

$\mathcal{V}$
EMERGERS

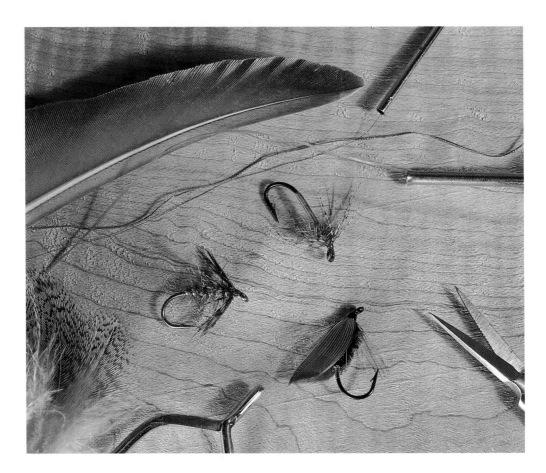

Introduction To Emergers

There was once a clear line between dry flies and nymphs; now that line often fades or disappears altogether. Most of the flies in this gray slot between nymph and dry fly are called "emergers," because the insects they imitate are emerging from their nymphal shucks. This gossamer time-slice of an insect's overall life span is now recognized as important—during these minutes, even seconds, aquatic

Hatching Mayfly

Skip Morris

insects are often at their most available and most defenseless, and trout seem to have caught on to this long before anglers did.

The traditional wet fly is a likely candidate as an emerger, though in its day, it was generally fished as one would fish a streamer. Today, the wet fly is making a return as an emerger. Soft hackles seem currently to be the most popular emergers, but there are others, and there will be others to come now that the importance of the partially hatched insect is understood.

TYING DIFFICULTY
1 is easy; 5 is difficult

March Brown Spider	2
Partridge and Orange	2
Leadwing Coachman	3

The March Brown Spider

In his book *The American Fly Tying Manual* Dave Hughes says, "This [the March Brown Spider] is the author's very favorite fly when it comes to searching a riffle or run at a time when no insects are hatching and no trout are rising." Personally, I have also found the March Brown Spider to be perfectly effective when trout *are* rising.

Deciding what length you want the hackle-fiber collar to be and finding the feather that will produce that length deserve some explaining. There seems to be quite a bit of leeway with regards to fiber length in a soft-hackle collar. The methods I will describe can produce a long, short, and moderate-length collar. To use a hackle gauge (normally used for dry-fly hackles), simply gauge the feather by its longest fibers. If you use a feather with fiber length that would normally suit a hook two sizes larger (for example, a size-8 hackle on a size-12 hook), you will have a long hackle collar. For a shorter hackle collar, gauge your feather to a hook one size larger; shorter yet, the same size as the hook you are using. You can also size the feather by setting its longest fibers along the hook; the fibers should reach from just behind the eye to the far edge of the bend; less than this will obviously produce shorter fibers. In a single hen-saddle or partridge-flank feather there are sections suitable for several different hook sizes—if you use the lowest, longest fibers on a given feather, they may suit a size-8 hook whereas the tip of that feather may fit a 14.

The method of winding hackle shown here is my favorite for soft-hackle flies—it is quick and easy to execute and the feather's stem is reinforced with thread turns. The Green and Partridge soft hackle demonstrates another, more common, approach. As Randall Kaufmann says in his book *The Nymph Tyer's Manual*, "hen saddle is easier to work with than the partridge that most soft-hackle patterns call for." Shown here is hen saddle; shown with the Green and Partridge is partidge flank—both are effective; use what you like. I consider the gold-tinsel rib optional; it seems a bit bright to me. Either dry-fly or standard nymph hooks can be used.

Fish the March Brown Spider as you would any soft-hackle fly—dead drift or coaxed weakly across current.

MARCH BROWN SPIDER

HOOK: Heavy wire and standard length or standard dry fly, sizes 18 to 10 (the hook shown is a Tiemco 3769).
THREAD: Orange 8/0 or 6/0.
RIB: Fine gold tinsel (oval or flat or use gold wire or omit the rib altogether).
BODY: hare's mask fur.
HACKLE: Brown partridge flank (or substitute hen saddle hackle as shown).

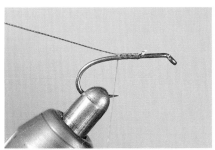

1. Start the thread three-quarters of the way up the shank, and tie in the tinsel using a light turn. Hold the tinsel above the shank at a slight angle as you spiral the thread tightly down both to the bend.

2. Dub up most of the shank with hare's mask fur. Wrap the tinsel up the body in several ribs. Secure the tinsel with thread wraps and trim the tinsel's end.

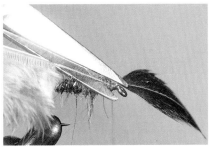

3. Select a partridge-flank or hen-saddle feather. Strip the fuzz from the base of the stem and then tie in the feather with a light turn just behind the eye. The feather should be projecting away from you and off the hook's eye with its stem projecting towards you and back. Ideally, the feather should be on its edge. Wrap the thread back a short distance to the front of the body. Trim closely the feather's stem.

4. Wrap the feather back in two (three at most) turns to the thread's end.

5. Take a couple of thread turns over the feather's tip, spiral the thread forward through the turns of hackle, and then snip out the hackle's tip.

6. Draw the fibers back using the triangle, and then build and complete the usual thread head.

The Partridge and Orange Soft Hackle

Here is truly a typical soft-hackle fly—floss body, hare's mask thorax, partridge-flank hackle. Its close cousins include the Partridge and Yellow and Partridge and Green.

You can simply start with thread, tie in the floss, wrap the floss, and secure the end of the floss with the thread. But I prefer to use single-strand floss in a floss bobbin for the first part of tying the Partridge and Orange because the floss bobbin makes it easier to build up the abdomen and is faster overall. The hackling method shown here is an alternate to the method demonstrated for the March Brown Spider; also, I will demonstrate with a feather that has been stripped on one side, which will create a sparsely dressed fly, but you *can* leave both sides of the feather intact as demonstrated with the March Brown Spider.

For more on selecting and sizing the hackle feather, hook choices, and fishing soft-hackle flies, see the previous section titled "The March Brown Spider."

PARTRIDGE AND ORANGE SOFT HACKLE

HOOK: Heavy wire and standard length or standard dry fly, sizes 18 to 10 (the hook shown is an Eagle Claw D57).
THREAD: Orange 8/0 or 6/0 and orange single-strand floss.
ABDOMEN: Orange floss.
THORAX: Hare's mask fur, dubbed short and thick.
HACKLE: Brown partridge flank.

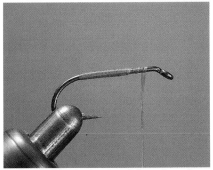

1. Start with single-strand floss in a floss bobbin. Start the floss, as you would thread, about two-thirds up the shank. Wrap a layer to the bend, then a second back to the starting point. Wind the floss forward another turn or two. (You can add two more layers of floss over the first two if you desire a thick abdomen; with the floss bobbin this is quick work.)

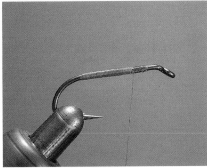

2. Start the tying thread over the extra turn of the floss at the front of the abdomen. Trim the ends of both the floss and the thread.

3. Dub a thick, short abdomen.

4. Draw back the fibers from the sides of a partridge-flank feather leaving the tip exposed. For a sparse soft-hackle fly, strip the fibers from one side of the feather. Shown are two feathers with their fibers drawn back, ready to be tied in; on the left is a whole feather and on the right, a feather with one side stripped.

5. Using the light turn, tie in the feather about 1/8" behind the eye. Ideally, the feather should be on its edge, cupped surface facing back, its tip towards you and forward, its bulk away from you and slanting back.

6. Trim off the tip of the feather. Advance the thread forward to just behind the eye. Wrap the feather forward two turns (three at most for either a whole feather or a half-stripped feather). Draw back the fibers using the triangle, build, whip finish, and add head cement to a thread head.

The Leadwing Coachman

Wet flies were once supremely popular, but they came to seem primitive and outdated as anglers learned more about the aquatic insects upon which trout feed. In place of such wet flies as the Black Gnat, Gray Hackle Peacock, and Cowdung there came plausable nymph imitations such as the Atherton Medium, Trueblood Otter, and Stone-Fly Creeper. All that most anglers now recall of wet flies are images of weepy rods, three-fly casts, and swift, unnatural fly retrieves.

But how accurate is that image? *Trout*, written by Ray Bergman and first published in 1952, then considered virtually the bible of trout fishing, says that "One of the most important methods of fishing the wet fly is the 'natural drift.'" Bergman goes on to explain that natural drift is what we now call dead drift, and dead drift is today generally considered a sophisticated, natural way to fish an artificial fly. Perhaps the wet fly hasn't such a crude history after all.

But if we forget history and look at the flies themselves, do they resemble real trout-food insects? With what we now know about aquatic insects, the answer appears to be yes. My friend Dave Hughes has long been a follower of the wet fly; he is one of those rare fellows who never gave it up. Dave sees the wet fly's obvious resemblence to a drowned winged insect, but he also sees more. From his studies into entomology, Dave found that some mayflies emerge from their shucks well under the surface; this leaves a fully winged adult swimming upwards—sound anything like a wet fly? Some caddisfly adults actually dive underwater to lay their eggs, and these too make fine models for the wet fly (though a diving caddis would probably be more a submerger than an emerger).

The Leadwing Coachman is a favorite of Dave's. He usually coaxes it weakly across the current or fishes it dead drift.

LEADWING COACHMAN

HOOK: Heavy wire, regular length, sizes 16 to 10 (the hook shown is a Partridge L2A).
THREAD: Black 8/0 or 6/0.
TAG: Gold tinsel (optional nowadays).
BODY: Peacock herl.
HACKLE: Brown hen neck.
WING: Natural gray duck-quill sections.

WRAPPING A TAG

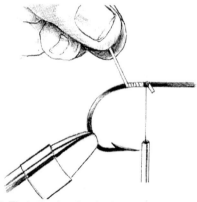
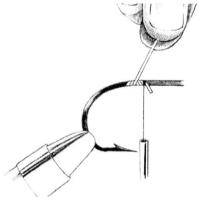

1. Start the thread just ahead of the bend. At the bend, tie in a section of gold tinsel at a slight angle, long end back and away, short end forward and towards you. Trim the short end if necessary.

Wrap the tinsel in a few close turns down the bend, and then wind the tinsel forward in close turns to its tie-in point. Secure the tinsel under a few tight thread turns, and then trim the tinsel. With that, the tag is complete. (Or just skip the tag altogether.)

1. Tie in the tinsel at the bend. Wrap the tinsel down the bend in a few close turns, neither overlapping nor spacing turns.

2. Reverse the wrapping direction of the tinsel and wrap it forward over the first turns. Again, the edges of the turns should just touch. Upon reaching the thread, secure the tinsel's end with tight thread turns.

2. Use the pinch to tie in two or three (depending on hook size) peacock herls at the bend. Trim the herls' ends. Spin the herls around the thread and wind this herl-thread rope up the shank. Secure the herls with thread turns about 1/8" back from the eye. Trim the ends of the herls.

3. Select a hackle that is, by dry-fly standards, slightly small for your hook size; that is, a size-11 hackle on a size-12 hook. If you are measuring hackle-fiber length against the hook, the fibers should be *slightly* short of 1 1/2 times the gape. Strip the fibers from the hackle's base. Advance the thread 1/16" and tie in the hackle. Snip off the hackle's stem, and return the thread to the front of the body.

4. Wind the hackle back in two to four close turns to the front of the body.

5. Secure the hackle's tip with two thread turns, and then spiral the thread forward through the hackle to just behind the hook's eye. Snip out the Hackle's tip.

6. Stroke back the hackle fibers. Take two or three thread turns back over the fibers to set them sweeping back.

7. Use the wing pinch to tie in a matched pair of duck-quill sections; the sections should be about one-half to three-quarters as wide as the gape. The sections should be cupped together, long edge up (long edge down is optional). There is room for personal preference regarding wing length—wings may end at the far edge of the bend, or they may extend slightly beyond. Trim the butts and build a thread head over them. Complete the thread head as usual.

VI
TINY NYMPHS

Introduction To Tiny Nymphs

Most anglers are uneasy about fishing tiny dry flies, and terrified about fishing tiny nymphs. But in truth, tiny nymphs are often *easier* to fish than tiny dry flies. I once wrote a magazine article that explained all the ins and outs behind this statement. Simply put, the toughest thing about fishing the tiny dry fly is seeing such a speck, but the tiny nymph is usually fished below a bright, highly visible strike indicator, and that indicator tells the angler all that is needed. In slow or still water, a straight line and leader telegraphs the take of a tiny nymph—easy.

But all this misses the real point, which is that trout often feed on tiny nymphs, larvae, and pupae to the exclusion of all else, so the angler must offer up a reasonable imitation or expect little action. In the end, the trout determine the real importance of tiny nymphs.

Many orders that include big insects also include tiny ones—*Hexagenia* mayflies can be fully eleven times as long as mayflies of the family *Caenidae*; caddis can range from a length of three millimeters to thirty; some midges are too small to be imitated on any fly hook, while imitations of others may require a hook of size 8. And there are yet other orders that include big and tiny. Logic might suggest that if there are big mayflies and tiny mayflies, the trout would surely prefer the big, but it doesn't work that way. For whatever reason—availability, familiarity, perhaps even taste—trout often lock in on one insect and refuse all else; if that insect is tiny, your imitation had better be tiny too.

The nymphs tied in this section are good examples, but there are many other nymph patterns that are tied tiny. In fact, most tiny nymphs are simply standard patterns tied on tiny hooks—for example, though I usually tie my Skip Nymphs in sizes twelve to sixteen, I also tie them in sizes twenty and even twenty-two.

Magnification can be especially useful for the tying of tiny nymphs. Even if you use magnification at no other time, strongly consider it here. Use tiny amount of materials for tiny nymphs—a wisp of dubbing, a single peacock herl for a thorax. And watch proportions—rather than looking like a ball of fur, a size-twenty Gold Ribbed Hare's Ear should have the same silhouette as a size-twelve. Having tried a few of the frail "midge" threads, I now use 8/0 for all but the very smallest hooks, hooks of size 26 and smaller. The trick is to use the fewest possible turns of thread.

TYING DIFFICULTY
1 is easy; 5 is difficult

Brassie	**2**
Copper Core Rick's Caddis	**3**
Cream Soft Hackle	**3**
Serendipity	**4**
Tiny Pheasant Tail	**4**

The Brassie

The Brassie can be tied in a wide range of sizes, but because it is so simple—just a bit of wire and a bit of dubbing—it makes an especially good tiny fly. Besides, the Brassie looks like a chironomid larva, and these are usually tiny. There isn't a lot of metal in this pattern, but there isn't much to add buoyancy or bulk, so the Brassie sinks well regardless of hook size. The Brassie also resembles some case-building caddis larvae, some small, some large.

The Brassie was created by Gene Lynch. Fish it well down, usually in streams.

BRASSIE

HOOK: Heavy wire, regular shank, 1X long, or 2X long, sizes 20 to 10 (the hook shown is an Eagle Claw D57).
THREAD: Black 8/0 or 6/0.
ABDOMEN: Copper wire, size is dependant upon hook size.
THORAX: Muskrat fur with guard hairs.

1. Start the thread about one-quarter down the shank from the eye. Secure one end of some copper wire at the thread's starting point with tight thread turns. Lift the wire slightly above the shank and spiral the thread down both to the bend. The thickness of the wire will determine both the fly's sink rate and the thickness of its abdomen, so chose with this in mind.

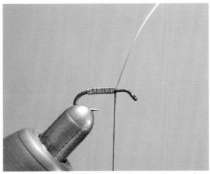

2. Advance the thread to its starting point; wind the wire in close tight turns to that point and secure it with tight thread turns. Trim the wire closely.

3. Dub a short thorax of muskrat; leave the guard hairs intact. Build and complete a thread head. You can pick out some of the fur and guard hairs with a hatpin, scissors' tip, or a bodkin. If the guard hairs are too long, trim them to length.

The Copper-Core Rick's Caddis

The Rick's Caddis is about as simple as a nymph gets—all dubbing. But the shape of a real caddis lava is simple too. The "Rick's" comes from the fly's originator, my friend Rick Hafele. Rick is a professional entomologist and fly-fishing author. He ties the Rick's Caddis in all sorts of colors—tan, brown, olive, gray—but the original was bright green, to imitate the *Rhyacophila* caddis larva common to the Deschutes River. Rick normally ties the Rick's Caddis on hooks of size 16 through 10, but sometimes he ties it much smaller than this to imitate a tiny larva.

Its utter simplicity makes the Rick's Caddis ideal as a tiny fly. You may have already tied the Copper-Core Pheasant Tail described in the section on mayfly nymphs. The Copper-Core Pheasant Tail was tied mostly with copper, but because the setting of the legs is easiest and neatest with thread, the switch was made; the Copper-Core Rick's Caddis is so simple that wire can be used throughout. As with the Copper-Core Pheasant Tail, the copper wire adds weight while adding little bulk—valuable in a tiny nymph.

Fish the Copper-Core Rick's Caddis well down, dead drift.

COPPER-CORE RICK'S CADDIS

HOOK: Heavy wire, regular shank or 1X long, sizes 20 to 10 (the hook shown is a Partridge L2A).
THREAD: In place of thread, fine copper wire.
ABDOMEN: Natural or synthetic dubbing in green, olive, tan, brown, black, cream.
THORAX: Natural hare's mask (or dyed, if that matches the natural).

1. Cut off a length of copper wire and start it, as you would thread, about 1/16" behind the eye. Wrap the wire in close turns down the shank to the bend. Spin dubbing onto the wire; you can wax the wire if you wish. You can also wind the wire forward up the shank and back to the bend again to add weight before adding dubbing.

2. Wrap the wire in close turns partway down the bend. With a little luck (and of course, a little practice), the dubbing will reach the hook just as you reverse the winding direction of the wire. Dub an abdomen up the bend and shank, but leave room for a short thorax.

3. Dub a short thorax of hare's mask.

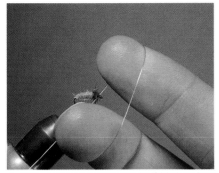

4. Secure the wire with two half hitches just behind the eye (you can actually whip finish the wire if you prefer). Trim the wire (but not with the tips of good scissors), and then add head cement.

The Cream Soft Hackle and the Spiraled Hackle

Esoteric language always caries with it the risk of burdensome and needless terms—must each field really have a name for every minor part and procedure? The term "spiraled hackle" must be near that line between useful and unnecessary. I chose to coin "spiraled hackle" because there are a lot of soft-hackle flies being tied these days, and this technique is valuable for their tying; so in order to keep it distinct from other hackling techniques, and because it accomplishes what others cannot, I gave it its own name.

The spiraled hackle allows you to use long fibers to make short collars. It is a technique that can be used on any soft-hackle fly, but it is especially useful for tiny flies. I'm sure the spiraled hackle has other useful applications beyond soft-hackle flies, but I haven't explored any yet.

The Cream Soft Hackle is only an example; any soft-hackle fly can be tied tiny. For more on hooks and fishing techniques for soft-hackle flies, refer to the section titled "The March Brown Spider."

CREAM SOFT HACKLE

HOOK: Heavy wire and standard length or standard dry fly,
    sizes 20 to 10 (the hook shown is a Mustad 3906).
THREAD: White 8/0.
HACKLE: Gray partridge flank (or substitute gray
    hen-saddle hackle).
BODY: Cream badger underfur (or substitute), dubbed.

1. Start the thread at midshank. Draw out the fibers along one side of the feather until the tips are squared. Strip off the fibers. Measure the fibers against the hook; note the point at which the fibers are equal to twice the shank length. Using the pinch, tie in the fibers with their measured point at midshank. Trim the fibers' butts.

2. Wrap the thread forward in close, tight turns over the fibers. As you do this, the fibers will slide around the shank and be distributed. If fibers slip behind the thread, a split second of thread slack will catch them; otherwise use plenty of constant thread tension. Wrap the thread to just short of the eye.

3. Spiral the thread back to the bend and dub a tapered body. The thread should now be just behind the partridge fibers that are projecting forward.

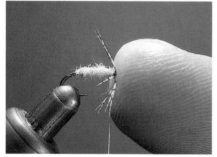

4. Push your right-hand fingertip straight into the hook's eye. This will spread the fibers away from the eye a bit.

5. Slide your right-hand fingertip along the fibers from various angles until the fibers are all stroked back. Grasp the fibers with your left-hand thumb tip and fingertip to hold them out of the way as you build a thread head. Complete the thread head as usual.

The Serendipity

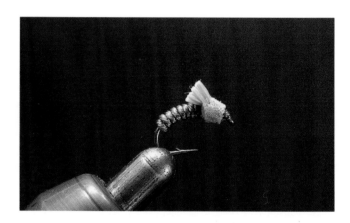

This fly was a bit of a mystery to me for some time. With a bit of snooping, I found that most Oregon anglers were fishing it dead drift in the surface film, but then a friend told me,"it's a killer down deep in the riffles on a dropper system." I couldn't find a pattern for the Serendipity in print, but when I perused the fly-fishing catalogs I saw pictures of flies called Serendipities that varied in body, head, and wing. Then I heard that the Serendipity had come out of Blue Ribbon Flies, so I wrote a letter containing a long list of questions to Craig Mathews along with an apology for pestering him with so many questions. Craig was kind enough to answer them all, and from those answers comes the information that follows.

Ross A. Merigold introduced the Serendipity to Mathews around 1988. It is generally considered an imitation of caddis and midge larvae and pupae. It can be tied with a trimmed-hair head or the hair can be trimmed closely and covered with thread for a thread head (Craig prefers the former approach, and that is the one that seems to be winning out). The Serendipity is fished both deep, and up in the surface film.

SERENDIPITY

HOOK: Heavy-to-regular wire, regular length, straight or humped shank, sizes 24 to 14 (the hook shown is a Tiemco 2457).
THREAD: 8/0 or 6/0 in a color to match the body.
BODY: Z-lon, twisted. Colors include tan, gray, olive, red, and brown.
HEAD and WING: Natural gray deer hair.

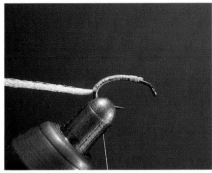

1. Start the thread about two-thirds up the shank. Use the pinch to tie in the Z-lon. Lift the Z-lon slightly above the shank under moderate tension, and then spiral the thread tightly down both it and the shank; continue spiraling the thread down the bend a bit.

2. Take a few tight turns of thread, and then spiral it back to its starting point. Twist the Z-lon tightly and wrap it up the bend and shank to the thread's starting point; continue to twist the Z-lon as you wrap it. Secure the Z-lon with thread turns, and trim the Z-lon's end.

3. Comb a small bunch of deer hair, trim off its tips, and then tie it in atop the hook at the front of the body using a light turn. The hairs' butts should project back, and the trimmed tips should project forward. Spiral the thread forward through the trimmed hair tips; this should spin the tips around the shank. Just behind the eye, draw the tips firmly back, and then whip finish the thread and trim it.

4. Hold the hairs' butts under light tension, slip the tips of your scissors in, and snip the hairs' butts at a slight angle as shown, the remaining stubs should be about equal in length to one-third the body's length.

5. Using a razor blade, scissors, or both, trim the hair butts to a rounded head as shown. If necessary, trim away some of the butt hairs to leave a neat wing case over the body. Add head cement to the whip finish.

The Tiny Pheasant Tail

In the section on mayfly nymphs, we explored the tying of a Pheasant Tail using copper wire in place of thread. You can do that here too; it's a good way to add weight. But here, we will explore the conventional approach to tying the Pheasant Tail on a tiny hook.

I searched for another mayfly-nymph imitation that has made its mark in tiny sizes, something new to show you, something other than the Pheasant Tail again. But every avenue I explored took me back to the Pheasant Tail—it seems to be everyone's first tiny mayfly-nymph choice. That shouldn't have surprised me. Of course I could have described it here only, but the Pheasant Tail is terribly popular in larger sizes too, and the techniques differ between the large and tiny. So in the end, I decided that to offer the Pheasant Tail from two different perspectives was to do right by the reader, by you.

I have often fished a tiny Pheasant Tail as a dropper with a heavily weighted stonefly-nymph imitation on the point. This makes sense in waters that hold lots of stoneflies and tiny mayflies such as the pale morning duns and little olives. It's a deadly combination. Usually the trout take the big stone in heavy stonefly water and the Pheasant Tail everywhere else. That, of course, is exactly how it's supposed to work, but it still amazes me every time it does.

Another good place for a tiny Pheasant Tail is right up at the surface during a hatch. A dry-fly or yarn strike-indicator makes this easy and effective.

For more about the Pheasant Tail, see "The Copper Core Pheasant Tail" in the section on mayfly nymphs.

TINY PHEASANT TAIL

HOOK: Regular to heavy wire, standard length or 1X long,
    sizes 16 to 22 (the hook shown is a Daiichi 1550).
THREAD: Brown 8/0.
TAIL: Pheasant-tail fibers.
RIB: Fine copper wire.
ABDOMEN: Pheasant-tail fibers.
THORAX: Peacock herl.
WING CASE: Pheasant-tail fibers.
LEGS: none.

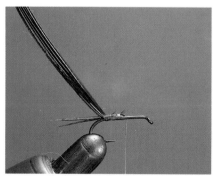

1. Start the thread at midshank; use the pinch to tie in a few pheasant-tail fibers there. Lift the fibers and spiral the thread down them to the bend. Fold the butts back and secure them at the bend with thread turns.

2. Tie in some copper wire at the bend. Wrap the thread up the shank and wire to just past midshank. Wrap the pheasant butts forward to just past midshank. Secure the butts there with tight thread turns. Trim the butts.

3. Using the pinch, just ahead of midshank, tie in about six pheasant-tail fibers projecting back. Tie in a short-fibered peacock herl. Trim the butts of both the pheasant and peacock.

4. Wrap the herl forward in close turns. Secure the herl just behind the eye with thread turns. Trim the herl.

5. Spiral the wire up the abdomen in four to six ribs. Continue spiraling the wire through the herl thorax in two or three turns to just behind the eye. Secure the wire with tight thread turns, and then trim the wire.

6. Pull the pheasant fibers forward and down to form a wing case. Secure the fibers at the eye with tight thread turns. Trim the fibers and complete the usual thread head. No legs—they are usually omitted on tiny Pheasant Tails.

VII

LAKE NYMPHS

Introduction To Lake Nymphs

It's tough being a dragonfly nymph in a water feature; just ask Linda (whose *true* gender, incidently, remains to me a mystery.) "Water feature" is a landscaper's name for a pond. My wife Carol is a full-time veterinarian, but a would-be landscaper, so she picked up the lingo and began unconsciously referring to our tiny, simple concrete pond as a water feature. I find the term pretentious, but I suspect Linda is used to it, so I'll use it here.

A month or so after our water feature was lowered into its earth-hole and filled with water, mosquito pupae showed up, hanging and squirming about the surface. Unfortunately, these are of only minor importance to trout and fly fishers, but I watched them with mild interest and waited for other life to appear.

A couple of months after that, almost overnight, the mosquito pupae all but disappeared—I could find only a few very tiny ones—and something much bigger seemed to dart from the concrete sides at my approach. I discovered that there were about eight big spider-shaped insects that shot for cover with remarkable speed: dragonfly nymphs. I caught one up in my insect net and took it along to a get-together with my friend Dave Hughes and entomologist Rick Hafele. "They've eaten all my mosquito pupae," I said.

"When they run out of other things to eat, they'll eat each other," said Rick.

"I had an aquarium once," said Dave. "I put in three dragonfly nymphs and about a hundred and fifty scuds. In almost no time I wound up with only one incredibly fat, bloated, barely able-to-move dragonfly nymph—no scuds, no other dragonfly nymphs."

By observing our water feature I have learned a lot about dragonfly nymphs; here are the primary points: They are deadly predators; they can move with impressive speed (though they often move slowly); and (though I have come to this conclusion through evidence rather than actually observing the behavior) they are active much of the time in order to satisfy their gluttony. This last point in particular stresses the importance of dragonfly nymphs as trout food—what could

be more interesting to trout than big, corpulent mouthful nymphs frequently out from cover and on the prowl?

Linda is bigger now, and all the other dragonfly nymphs have disappeared. It's grim to think of devouring one's siblings in order to survive, but I feel confident that any of her brothers or sisters would have done it. In the end, only Linda remains. And though I can't prove that her siblings didn't succumb to predators or sickness, she has jumped from what women call the juniors category to what they call plus-size; her new proportions are a grim reminder of the hard evidence.

Damselflies are related to dragonflies. Dragonfly nymphs are stout; damselfly nymphs are slender; yet somehow there is a resemblance. I have never seen heavy populations of dragonfly nymphs, but I have seen dense hatches of damselfly nymphs, an olive mass sculling shore-ward. At such times, a damselfly-nymph imitation can fetch a very good price should you have extras when other anglers have none.

In fall, and even winter, backswimmers and waterboatmen kick about with long paddle legs, finding food and dodging trout. Leeches inhabit many lakes and search for hosts as trout search for them.

There are other creatures important to the lake fisher—caddisflies and mayflies in particular—and the tying of their imitations is described in other sections.

TYING DIFFICULTY
1 is easy; 5 is difficult

TDC	**2**
Janssen's Marabou Leech	**2**
Daedalian Damsel	**3**
Taylor Dragonfly Nymph	**3**
Backswimmer	**4**
Woven Dragonfly Nymph	**4**

The TDC

Developed by biologist Richard B. Thompson, the TDC's unusual name is an acronym for "Thompson's Delectable Chironomid." I've used this fly successfully for years on Pacific northwest lakes.

In his little gem of a book *Western Streamside Guide*, Dave Hughes describes well the techniques for fishing the TDC:

> There are two tactics that work well with midge pupal patterns. The first is to use a 12- to 15-foot leader and a strike indicator. Dress the leader with floatant to within a few inches of the fly. Then cast out and work it back very slowly. The idea is to let the fly hang just below the surface. This represents the pupa just before it emerges.

> The second tactic is to use a longer leader, and slightly weighted fly. Cast long. Let the fly sink patiently. Then bring it in with a retrieve that raises it slowly toward the surface. This represents the pupa as it rises toward the top for emergence. Leaders as long as 20 to 25 feet are used by experts at this method.

My experience is greatest with the first tactic Dave describes—it works.

I've noticed that chironomids often run larger in lakes than in streams. Chironomid pupa are usually tiny in streams—hooks of size 18, 20, and even smaller may be required—whereas lake chironomid pupa may be appropriately imitated on hooks of size 10—even 8.

TDC

HOOK: Regular or heavy wire, regular shank or 1X long, sizes 18 to 8 (the hook shown is a Dai-Riki 075).
THREAD: Black 8/0 or 6/0.
RIB: Fine silver tinsel or wire (I prefer the wire).
ABDOMEN: Black wool or fur dubbing (I prefer the dubbing).
THORAX: Short. The same material as the abdomen but thicker.
HEAD: White ostrich herl.

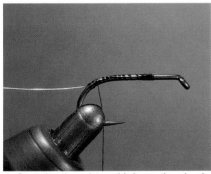

1. Start the thread two-thirds up the shank. Use a light turn to tie in the wire. Hold the wire up slightly as you spiral the thread down it and the shank to just beyond the bend.

2. Dub a slender abdomen up two-thirds of the shank.

3. Dub a bit further for a thick, short thorax. Wrap the wire up the abdomen and thorax in six to ten ribs. Secure the wire under thread and trim the wire's end.

4. Tie in an ostrich herl, trim its end, spin the herl and thread together, and wrap the herl forward two or three turns. Unravel the remaining herl and secure it under thread turns. Trim the herl, build a thread head, add a whip finish, trim the thread, and coat the head with head cement.

The Janssen Marabou Leech

There isn't much to a leech, at least it seems that way when you look at one, so it shouldn't be any surprise that there isn't much to a leech imitation. And because leech imitations are so simple, nobody seems to worry much about specific patterns. The leech fly in *Fly Patterns of Yellowstone*, by Craig Mathews and John Juracek, is the only fly that lacks a neatly listed pattern. Instead, the authors describe its components as follows:

Simple patterns such as a marabou tail and body, marabou tail with leech yarn body or, even simpler yet, a leech yarn body frizzed out all produce well.

Hal Janssen's Marabou Leech is a well-established leech imitation. It can be tied in black, olive, brown, gray, or tan.

Leeches are found in lakes and very slow streams. Fish the Janssen Marabou Leech well down, with a steady swimming motion.

MARABOU LEECH

HOOK: Heavy wire, at least 4X long, sizes 10 to 4 (the hook shown is a Tiemco 300).
THREAD: 3/0 of a color to match the wing and tail.
TAIL: Marabou fibers.
WING: Marabou fibers.
HEAD: Marabou fibers.

1. Start the thread about one-third up the shank from the bend. Strip a bunch of fibers from the side of a marabou plume. Measure the fibers against the hook, and then tie in the fibers at the one-third point; the fibers should project from the bend one full shank's length. Spiral the thread down the shank and marabou to the bend. Wrap the thread in close turns back up one-third of the shank. trim the butts of the marabou closely.

2. One-third up the shank from the bend tie in another bunch of fibers. These too should be a full shank's length.

3. Wrap the thread up the butts of this second bunch until the thread is two-thirds up the shank. Trim the butts of the marabou closely. Measure and tie in another bunch of marabou, and then trim and bind its butts.

4. Halfway between this two-thirds bunch and the eye, measure and tie in another bunch of marabou. Trim its butts and then, halfway between this bunch and the eye, tie in another measured bunch, but don't trim the butts on this one. To review, there is now a tail at the bend, a marabou wing bunch one-third of the shank up from the bend, a second wing bunch two-thirds up the shank, a third bunch halfway between the second and the eye, and a fourth halfway between the third and the eye.

5. There should remain, between the last bunch and the eye, roughly 3/16" of shank. Spin the marabou and thread together, and then wrap this marabou-thread rope up to just behind the eye. Trim the butts, and then build and complete a thread head.

The Daedalian Damsel

One evening, Bob Guard and Ken Fujii decided to construct the perfect damselfly-nymph imitation. It was well that they started early and were willing to stay up late, because even with their years of fishing the damselfly hatch and fly tying behind them it was a formidable task. They began with these ground rules: It must be easy and quick to tie, durable, simple, and it must have all the most significant features of real damsel nymphs. After trying all the conventional approaches, they explored their most fanciful notions and produced flies that ranged from ornate, exact replicas to ragged bits of green. They gave up on the idea that any artificial could create the same sinewy sculling motion of a swimming damsel, but they did conclude that a soft, fluffy fly would pulse and look alive in water and in that way, suggest movement. What they came up with is clever, it follows their ground rules, and it works. In retrospect, it is surprising that they came up with the Daedalian Damsel in a single evening.

Normally it is easy enough to find adequately long marabou strands; just use the ones nearest the base of the plume. Remember that the more fibers you use, the less of their length it will take to cover the shank and the more you will have remaining for wing case and legs; a section covering 1 1/2" to 2" of the stem is usually about right. Another marabou saver is to slightly spread the marabou turns over the front half of the shank. Occasionally you will get marabou that is short, in which case you can simply wrap the marabou to the eye and then spread it for legs, without forming the wing case at all. Another trick is to use 3/0 thread and simply leave its end loose at the bend; then you can use the end of the thread as ribbing in place of the copper wire. If you wet the marabou, it is easiest to handle.

Damselfly nymphs swim in a slow, snakelike manner with occasional pauses; make your Daedalian Damsel do the same.

"Daedalian" comes from "Daedalus," a character from Greek mythology. Daedelus created something ingenious—a labyrinth—did something stupid—got himself and his son imprisoned in it—and then escaped by creating something ingenious—wings that strapped to the arms. So "Daedalian" should mean "something ingenious followed by something stupid followed by something ingenious", but the stupid part and the second ingenious part have been discarded leaving "Daedalian" to mean "ingenious"; for that, the Daedalian Damsel is well named.

DAEDALIAN DAMSEL

HOOK: Regular to heavy wire, 3X or 4X long, humped or straight shank, sizes 12 to 8 (the hook shown is a Gamakatsu F-16).
THREAD: A color to match the marabou in 8/0 or 6/0.
RIB: Fine copper wire.
ABDOMEN, THORAX, WING CASE, LEGS: Olive or brown marabou fibers.

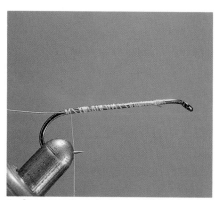

1. Start the thread about 1/8" behind the eye, tie in the copper wire using a light turn. Hold the copper wire along the near side of the shank as you spiral the thread down it and the shank to the bend.

2. Strip some long marabou fibers from the base of a plume. Using the pinch, secure them at the bend with two tight turns of thread.

3. Lift the fibers and spiral the thread forward to about 1/16" behind the eye. Twist the marabou slightly, and then wrap it up the shank to the end of the thread (about 1/8" behind the eye).

4. Secure the butts of the marabou atop the shank with tight thread turns. Wrap the wire up about three-quarters of the shank in four or five open spirals.

5. Pull the marabou's butts firmly back and secure them with a turn of wire atop the shank. Continue spiraling the wire forward to about 1/16" behind the eye. Secure the wire with thread turns, and then trim its end.

6. Pull the marabou's butts forward atop the shank and secure them with tight thread turns. Pinch the butts with one hand and use the thumbnail of your other to rip them to length. The trick is to pinch the marabou just tight enough to allow some fibers to break at the thread and others to shear off longer, a ragged, modestly thick effect. A few rips can be easier than one. If you have trouble ripping, use scissors.

When you have enough ripped butts for legs, trim away the excess from atop the shank. Remember that damselflies have short legs and that they carry their legs well bent which makes the legs appear shorter yet.

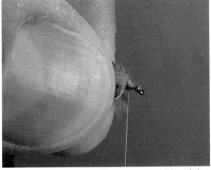

7. Pull half the butts firmly to one side of the shank and half to the other (if you think you have too many butts, trim out some more). Wrap the thread back over the butts to secure them along and projecting out from the sides (it can help to secure one bunch at a time). Build a thread head, add a whip finish, trim the thread, and add head cement.

8. Here is how the butt-legs should appear from a top view.

The Backswimmer

For their similarities, backswimmers and waterboatmen are usually lumped together, at least by fly fishers, but both insects are of the order *Hemiptera*, so they are close cousins and probably have a sense of family anyway—surely they would take no offense at this lumping. What backswimmers and waterboatmen have in common are their long oar-like legs that scoot them along. Since both insects must take air from the surface, they must be able to dive quickly away from predators that attack them there. Actually, backswimmers are fierce predators themselves. They feed on other insects and even tiny fish; in fact, a favorite entree is plant-eating waterboatmen—perhaps backswimmers and waterboatmen *would* take offense at being lumped.

Al Troth's Backswimmer is a fine imitation of both back-swimmers and waterboatmen. Both insects carry a bubble of air under their wings (yes, they also have wings, but use them only as a last resort) and another under their abdomen; hence the tinsel of Al's Backswimmer. Al is currently leaning towards a change in this fly: round rubber strands for the oar-legs, in place of the biots. And though he would prefer olive strands, black seems the closest color currently available in fine diameter; Al feels that the benefits of the rubber strand outweigh the color limitations.

Backswimmers prefer the edges of lakes and ponds and move slowly under most circumstances, quickly when threatened. This leaves you plenty of latitude when imparting movement to your Backswimmer.

BACKSWIMMER

HOOK: Heavy wire, regular shank, 1X, or 2X long, sizes 16 to 10 (the hook shown is an Orvis 1524).

THREAD: Olive 8/0 or 6/0.

WEIGHT: Lead wire (optional).

BACK: Heavily barred wood-duck-flank feather (or mallard dyed wood-duck color) with a strip of clear plastic sheeting over it (such sheeting can be found in heavy sandwich or freezer bags and is often used for packaging and protective coverings).

RIB: Fine oval silver tinsel.

BODY: Dark olive dubbing (dyed hare's mask is shown).

LEGS: Dyed olive turkey biots (dyed goose biots for a substitute). (Al now feels that dark fine round rubber strand may be best.)

HEAD: The same fur as the body, dubbed full.

TOP OF HEAD: The same plastic strip that covers the back.

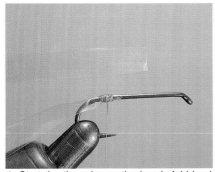

1. Start the thread near the bend. Add lead and thread bind it now, if you plan to use it. Build a tight, short thread layer. Tie in a strip of clear plastic sheeting at the bend as shown; the strip should be slightly more than half as wide as the gape.

2. Strip the fuzz from the base of a well-marked wood-duck feather (or a dyed-mallard substitute). Wet the base of the feather (to soften it so that it won't break when you soon pull it forward). At the bend, tie in the feather by its butt; the feather should be tied in up into the fibers a bit. Tie in the tinsel at the bend and secure it with tight thread turns. Trim the ends of both the wood duck and tinsel.

3. Dub heavily up half the shank. Tie in a turkey or goose biot on either side of the shank, at midshank, against the front of the body. The quills should project from their tie-in point about one shank's length and should curve back. Trim the butts of the biots.

As an option, tie in a rubber strand using the pinch; then crisscross the thread around the strand's base to set the ends out to the sides (see "The Girdle Bug"). Trim the quills' butts.

4. Dub behind the quills to force them out to the sides, slanting slightly back, and then dub a bit right in front of them to three-quarters up the shank. Spiral the tinsel to the back of the biots in a few ribs. You can keep the quills out of the way by manipulating them with your scissor's closed tips. Add another turn or two of tinsel in front of the biots, thread bind the tinsel, and then trim it.

5. Advance the thread to the hook's eye. Once more, wet the wood-duck feather at its tie-in point (so it won't break) and then pull it up and then flatly, firmly down over the top of the hook. Add tight thread turns at the eye (see "Wing-Case Construction" in section IX, "Basic Techniques"). Trim the tips of the wood duck.

6. Pull the plastic strip firmly up and then forward and down over the body. Secure the strip with tight thread turns. Do not cut the plastic strip yet.

7. Dub a small, short head. With the thread at the rear of the head, pull the end of the plastic strip back and secure it at the front of the body with tight thread turns (same approach as you just used to form the back, but in the opposite direction), and build and complete a thread collar.

Pull the end of the plastic strip firmly up and trim it closely. Add a whip finish, trim the thread, add head cement to the thread colar.

8. Here is a Backswimmer with rubber-strand legs. I find it easiest to tie in the legs first, and then dub all the body. When the fly is tied, trim the strands to length.

The Taylor Dragonfly Nymph

Marv Taylor is used to fishing for big, angler-wary trout; he often does so in the lakes around his Idaho home. He shared his years of lake-fishing experience in his book *Float-Tubes, Fly Rods and other essays*. In that book he describes the tying of the Taylor Dragonfly Nymph, a simple pattern with the outline and corpulence of a real dragon nymph.

Fish the Taylor Dragonfly nymph slowly along the bottom near weed beds; it can also be good on a fast retrieve.

TAYLOR DRAGONFLY NYMPH

HOOK: Heavy wire, 4X long, sizes 12 to 6 (the hook shown is an Eagle Claw D281).
THREAD: Brown 3/0.
TAIL: Three or four pheasant-tail fibers.
ABDOMEN: A football-shaped foundation of wool yarn (or a substitute) wrapped over with large, dark olive-brown chenille (if I can't get olive-brown, I just use brown).
HACKLE: Grizzly dyed dark olive green (or substitute dark olive or dark brown).
WING CASE: Pheasant-tail fibers.
THORAX: Small dark olive-brown chenille.

1. Start the thread at the bend and use the pinch to tie in three or four pheasant-tail fibers there as a short tail. Secure the fibers well, and then trim the fibers' butts. Advance the thread two-thirds up the shank and tie in the large chenille using the pinch. Lift the chenille slightly and spiral the thread down it to the bend. Trim the butts of the fibers.

2. Use the pinch to tie in some wool yarn at the bend. Wrap the wool into a football shaped hump covering the rear two-thirds of the shank. Secure the yarn with thread turns two-thirds up the shank and cut the yarn's end. Bind the wool all over with tight thread turns. (No need to build more than a modest hump; the chenille will provide bulk.)

3. Advance the thread. Wrap the chenille up the wool foundation and secure it with thread turns two-thirds up the shank. Trim the end of the chenille.

4. Tie in the hackle, trim its stem, and then wrap it forward in three close turns. Secure the hackle's tip under thread and trim the tip off.

5. Trim the hackle fibers away on top. Snip a bunch of fibers from a pheasant tail and tie them in atop the shank projecting back over the abdomen. Lift the fibers and trim them about one-third of the way back over the abdomen.

6. Advance the thread to just behind the eye. Tie in the small chenille just ahead of the hackle. Wrap the chenille forward, secure it under thread, trim the chenille's end.

7. Build a thread head; whip finish and trim the thread. trim the hackle fibers from beneath, and trim the chenille closely under the abdomen. Add head cement to the thread head.

The Woven Dragonfly Nymph

I've watched Darrel Martin tie his dragonfly nymph twice. The second time, Darrel described the steps in detail and answered all my questions. I had assumed by the look of it that the Woven Dragonfly Nymph would be time consuming to tie; it isn't. Actually, the version that Darrel tied for me is slightly simpler than the one he describes in his excellent book *Fly-Tying Methods*.

Though it may seem difficult, the woven body can be created quite easily and quickly; the trick is to cut the thread just before weaving, and to turn the vise away from you, so that you are sighting down the shank with the hook's bend nearest you, before you weave. Another trick is to make a template and use it to mark the leather before cutting out the under body. An old soft-leather shoe is a good source for the leather, but you can build up the under body in whatever manner you see fit. Darrel particularly likes the leather because it soaks up water and because it can be shaped by the placement and tightness of the thread wraps. You can buy a whole dyed rabbit pelt for the Woven Dragonfly's legs, or you can purchase a small bag of rabbit hide cut into strips for tying a pattern called a Zonker.

All dragonfly-nymph imitations are fished in lakes and slow streams and are made to swim slowly, quickly, or in tiny repeated bursts.

WOVEN DRAGONFLY NYMPH

HOOK: Heavy wire, 3X long (humped shank preferred), size 6 (the hook shown is a Daiichi 1270).
THREAD: Brown 3/0.
EYES: Brown vernille (chenille as a substitute).
UNDER BODY: Medium-soft leather.
ABDOMEN: Brown and chartreuse or brown and olive vernille, or ultra-chenille (chenille as a substitute).
LEGS: Brown rabbit fur in a dubbing loop.
WING CASE and TOP OF HEAD: A small body feather—hen saddle, partridge, etc.—glued to a lady's nylon stocking, or simply lacquered, and then trimmed leaving a "v" notch in its tip (a quill section coated with Tuffilm, or even swiss straw make good substitutes, as do other durable, flat materials).
THORAX: Any absorbent, brown dubbing.

1. Cover the shank with open spirals of thread. Cut two half-teardrop shapes as shown from medium-soft leather, and secure one on one side of the shank with tight thread turns. Secure the other piece of leather on the other side in the same manner. you can control the shape of the leather underbody with the tightness and placement of the thread turns.

2. Just behind the hook's eye, secure a length of brown vernille atop the shank by crisscrossing the thread over it and the shank. Bunch one end of the vernille up along the shank from behind and secure it with thread turns; the result should be a tiny loop. Do the same with the other end of the vernille. Trim the remaining ends and bind them. The photograph shows one eye formed, the other yet to be formed.

3. Spiral the thread back to the bend and tie in a length of brown vernille on one side of the shank and a length of chartreuse (or olive) vernille on the other. Whip finish the thread and cut it. Turn the vise so that its jaws are pointing away from you, and then weave the vernille into an abdomen as shown in the illustration. Pull back a bit on the vernille as you weave to keep the weaving tight.

Weaving an Abdomen

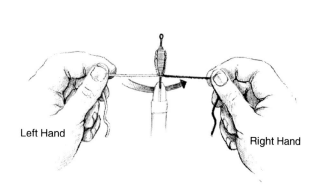

Left Hand

Right Hand

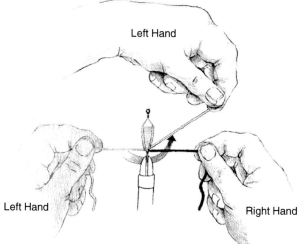

Left Hand

Left Hand

Right Hand

1. Start with your vise turned so that the hook points away from you. Hold one strand of vernille in your left hand and one in your right.

2. Swing your left hand, and the vernille, under the hook, and then to the hook's right side. Despite what you might think, you will continue to hold the vernille throughout the weaving process—you will not release it, nor will you switch either strand from one hand to the other.

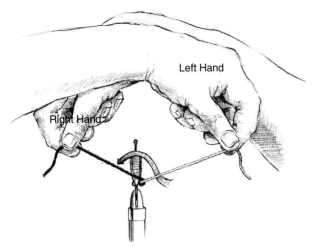

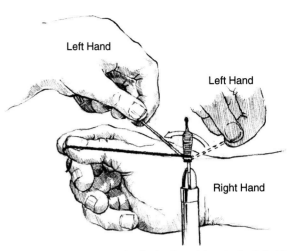

3. Swing your right hand across the top of the shank, under your left hand, to the left side of the hook.

4. Swing your left hand *under* the hook and then to the left side and back against the dark vernille. You now have your first woven lock on the right side of the under body.

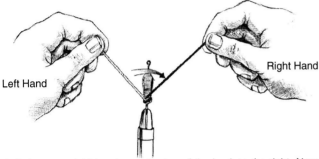

5. Swing your right hand over the top of the hook to the right. Now you have a lock on each side of the abdomen. Continue this sequence until you've completed the woven abdomen.

4. Clamp your hackle pliers onto the ends of the vernille; this frees your hands. Start the thread again over the ends of the vernille, add plenty of tight thread turns, and then trim the loose ends of the vernille and thread. Form a dubbing loop, carefully slip some rabbit fur into it, twist the loop tight, and wrap it forward in two or three turns. Secure the end of the loop with tight thread turns and trim. (See "Dubbing-Loop Collar" in section IX, "Basic Techniques."

5. Trim an elongated shape, with a "V" notch in its tip, from a body feather, the same shape as the feather on the needle shown. The feather should be lacquered, or glued to a lady's nylon stocking (see the next step, #6). Advance the thread to just behind the hook's eye and tie the feather in by its stem, projecting off the eye. Test the feather's length by folding it back—if it reaches back about 3/8" over the abdomen, fine; if not, adjust its length by tying it in further up or down its stem or by trimming the feather down.

6. Dub all around the thorax and eyes and end with the dubbed thread projecting immediately in front of the dubbing-loop legs, behind the eyes. Fold back the head-wing case feather and secure it with turns of dubbed thread. Angle the thread sharply under the eyes to the hook's eye. Build a small thread head, add a whip finish, add head cement. Another approach, which suits my style, is to build a thread collar behind the eyes, whip finish the collar, and add head cement to it, rather than advancing the thread to the hook's eye.

Darrel prefers that the feather that forms the wing case and head has a backing of nylon mesh from a lady's stocking. The stocking is lightly stretched over a needle-point hoop, and then a batch of feathers are glued to the mesh with P V C glue (glue used for P C V pipe). I've had good results using Dave's Flexament for this.

VIII

MISCELLANEOUS NYMPHS

Introduction To Miscellaneous Nymphs

"Miscellaneous" refers here to any artificial nymphs that fit none of the categories we've covered. Actually, most of the nymphs in this section could fit loosely into several categories. What does a trout believe it is taking in the Red Fox Squirrel Hair Nymph?—a mayfly nymph? a caddis larva? even, perhaps, a stonefly nymph? Who can say for certain? Indeed, the Red Fox Squirrel Hair Nymph resembles all these, and it must certainly be taken for each from time to time. Most of the time, however, it is likely taken as no more than something alive and edible and available. There is little to suggest that trout take seriously the study of entomology.

Nymphs such as the Red Fox Squirrel Hair Nymph and the Prince Nymph are often called searching nymphs or attractor nymphs because, as these names imply, they are used to search for and attract trout without imitating a specific insect. Neither of these names was used to head this section, however, because not all the nymphs here fall under them. Bead heads could be called searching or attractor nymphs, though they could just as easily be called bizarre nymphs.

Only two of the nymphs in this section are imitations of specific creatures: the San Juan Worm, which imitates an aquatic earthworm, and the Scud, which imitates a freshwater shrimp. These flies are listed here, along with the attrac-

tor nymphs, because they and the creatures they imitate fit none of the other categories I've listed. But worms and shrimp and attractor nymphs *do* fit into the catch-all category of "miscellaneous."

TYING DIFFICULTY
1 is easy; 5 is difficult

San Juan Worm	1
Woolly Worm	2
Girdle Bug	2
Red Fox Squirrel Hair Nymph	2
Bird's Nest	2
Prince Nymph	3
Zug Bug	3
Scud	3
The Bead Head	varies

The San Juan Worm

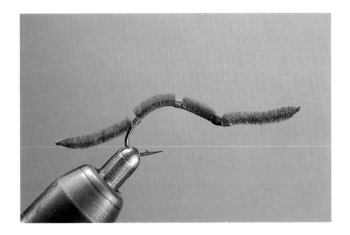

This is another of those flies that everyone seems to talk about, tie, and fish, but nobody seems sure as to exactly how it's tied. The method shown here is my favorite, but you will see plenty of others.

Rick Hafele, professional entomologist and fly-fishing author, tells me that the San Juan worm imitates an aquatic species of earthworm that is quite common. Its appearance is very close to that of the standard backyard earthworm—which may well explain the deadliness of the oft-mentioned boy with a bamboo stalk, a few feet of fishing line, and a worm on a hook. The San Juan Worm is often tied in red, but Rick says that the naturals are more of a brown or reddish brown.

These worms don't swim, so they should be fished dead drift.

SAN JUAN WORM

HOOK: Heavy wire, regular shank (I prefer a humped shank), sizes 16 to 8 (the hook shown is a Gamakatsu F-22).
THREAD: 3/0 in a color to match the Ultra Chenille or Vernille; for small hooks, 8/0 or 6/0 can be substituted.
EVERYTHING ELSE: Red, brown, or reddish-brown Ultra Chenille or Vernille.

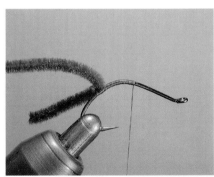

1. Start the thread at the rear of the shank (this takes a bit of guesswork on humped shanks, but an approximation is all that is required). Tie a length of vernille at the rear of the shank with a slim band of tight thread turns. The end of the vernille should extend back from its tie-in point about a shank's length. Lift the Vernille, and advance the thread to midshank.

2. Secure the Vernille at midshank with another slim thread band. Lift the Vernille and advance the thread again.

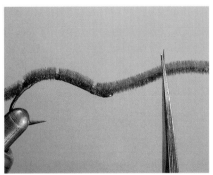

3. Secure the Vernille with a thread band again, right behind the eye. Whip finish and trim the thread on the last band. Trim the vernille so that it extends forward from its tie-in point about a shank's length.

4. Singe the ends of the Vernille with a flame to keep them from unraveling. Add head cement to the thread band at the eye.

The Woolly Bugger and an Exercise in Tying Efficiency

The Woolly Bugger is a simple, deadly fly that caught on fast. No one really knows what trout take it to be, but it works.

The "Learning From the Professional Tier" section in this book discusses the principles behind tying efficiency; with the Woolly Bugger you'll see those principles at work.

There are a number of ways to tie this fly. I'll briefly demonstrate a standard approach, and then show you my own approach incorporating the principles of tying efficiency.

The Woolly Bugger can be weighted or unweighted. Determining the size of the hackle is largely subjective.

Regardless of the hackle-fiber length you prefer, a dry-fly hackle gauge is a good tool for keeping this length consistent. I have vacillated somewhat on Woolly Bugger hackle-fiber length, but right now, as a general guide, I'd use a hackle with fibers appropriate for a hook one size larger than the hook I'm using if that hook is 4X long. The Woolly Bugger is usually fished with twitches for a swimming motion that makes the marabou pulse, come alive.

Is the Woolly Bugger a nymph? or is it a streamer? Depends on whom you ask. But to me it seems close enough to a nymph to be included in a nymph-tying book.

The Woolly Bugger was created by Russell Blessing.

BLACK WOOLLY BUGGER

HOOK: Heavy wire, 3X long and longer, sizes 14 to 2 (the hook shown is a Dai-Riki 700).
THREAD: Black 3/0 or a color to match the body.
WEIGHT: Lead wire (optional).
TAIL: One black marabou plume, but variations include many other colors. The tail's color usually matches the body's.
BODY: Black chenille, but variations now include almost every possible color.
HACKLE: Black, but variations now include a wide range of markings and colors.

1. A conventional approach to tying the Woolly Bugger: Here a marabou plume was tied in (shank length); the hackle was tied in by its tip; the chenille was tied in, wrapped, thread secured, and trimmed; and now the hackle is being palmered up the body. Simple. Now, let's explore another approach with an eye on efficiency.

2. With all your materials prepared (hackles sized and stripped at the base, hook barbs smashed, etc.) and all your materials and tools laid out (and all unnecessary materials and tools put away), start your thread just ahead of the bend; this allows you to work forward from this point so that you can work back again from the next point—you'll see. Dip your fingers into a bowl of water and stroke the water into a marabou plume (wetted marabou is always easier to handle than dry). Use the pinch to tie in the plume at the bend (the plume should extend from the bend one shank's length). After adding tight thread turns, lift the plume's butts, quickly spiral the thread up the shank to 1/8" behind the eye, lower the butts, and secure them using the pinch. This is a quick, efficient way to tie in the butts. Trim the butts closely with one snip (from the scissors you haven't and won't put down).

3. Since the thread is now at the *front* of the shank, it makes sense to tie in the next material from the front to the rear—in this case, copper wire. Use a light turn to tie in the *tip* of the wire 1/8" back from the eye. By tying in the tip, you will have no end to trim. Lift the wire slightly above the shank and spiral the thread down wire and shank to the bend. If you left the wire uncut, with the spool off the rear of the vise's jaws, the spool will keep the wire out of your way.

4. Since the thread is at the bend, it makes sense now to tie in the next material from rear to front—as you did with the marabou. Use the pinch to tie in some chenille at the bend. Tie in the chenille so that its end reaches *slightly* beyond the eye—less to trim, less waste. Slide your thumb and finger up the chenille and support its position atop the shank just behind the thread as you spiral the thread up the shank and chenille to about 1/8" behind the eye. Trim the chenille's stub end.

There is an even faster way to tie in the marabou, wire, and chenille—tie each in at the bend over just enough shank with just enough tight thread turns to really hold each material; then snip all the materials closely. The tradeoff is that you will have a bulge in the body at the bend, but if you don't mind that, you will save a little time on each fly, and that time adds up.

5. Take up a hackle (all the hackles you will be using during this session are already sized and stripped, remember?) and snip its bare stem to about 1/4" (most listings for this pattern call for saddle hackle, but if you've got some long, soft leftover rooster neck hackles why not use them? less waste, similar results). Dip the stem in the water to soften it. Tie in the hackle projecting out from the eye about 1/16" behind the eye.

6. Work the thread to 1/8" behind the eye. Wrap the chenille up the shank. If you work with a long piece of chenille, enough for a few flies, there will be less cutting; simply manipulate the long end so that it doesn't catch on bobbin, hackle, or hook point. Keep your grasp close to the hook though for tiny efficient orbits. Secure the end of the chenille with thread 1/8" behind the eye. Trim the chenille's end. (You still haven't set down your scissors I hope.)

  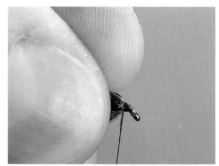

7. Advance the thread to 1/16" behind the eye, right at the hackle's tie-in point. Take just an extra fraction of a second to *swing* the hackle stem to a right angle to the shank—a sudden jerk or pressure applied all to one point on the stem could break it at this angle; wetting the stem helped by softening it. Wrap the hackle behind the thread's end. Take two or three close turns of hackle working rearward, then palmer the hackle down the chenille to the bend. Don't bother with hackle pliers—one more tool to pick up, and they aren't really necessary here anyway.

8. Snip the copper wire to length deep into your scissors's blades ("proper length" means minimal waste, just enough to do the job comfortably, something worked out by repetition; were your scissors in the correct hand to best accomplish this?). Take a turn of wire over the hackle's tip, release the tip, and take another turn over it. spiral the wire up the body to the eye.

9. Secure the wire with one tight thread turn. Draw down the bobbin to keep that turn tight as you use the triangle to draw back hackle fibers and wire. Build a thread head that wraps back a bit over the wire's end (this makes the wire's tie-in point very secure). Add a whip finish (one-handed of course because it's the fastest). Snip the hackle's tip, the thread and, deep into the scissors's blades, the wire. Finished.

Now it's time to hone technique: Where can you use fewer thread turns? Can you trade the scissors from hand to hand at key points for greater efficiency? What else can you do to streamline your technique for tying this fly?

The Girdle Bug

This one came very close to falling under the heading of stonefly-nymph imitations; anyone experienced with stonefly nymphs will require only a glance to confirm the similarity. Yet the Girdle Bug is only described in print as a stonefly nymph about half the time; the rest of the time it is described as an attractor nymph.

Perhaps the confusion over what the Girdle Bug does or does not imitate stems from the confusion concerning its dressing. After pouring over numerous books and catalogs, I have seen it listed with a tinsel rib, without a tinsel rib, with a light-brown under body, without an under body, with rubber-strand antennae, without antennae, with white rubber strands, with black rubber strands, with the strands evenly spaced over the shank, and with the strands at the front half of the shank only.

Even the name is in question. One book lumps the Girdle Bug and the Rubber Legs together as two names for one fly: "Rubber Legs-Girdle Bug." Another describes the Girdle Bug as "The same as the Rubber Legs except that it uses dark-colored rubber hackle." Yet another book clearly

calls for white rubber strands on the Girdle Bug. A prominent mail-order firm takes no chances concerning the question of rubber-strand color by calling it in their catalog the "Black Rubberlegs;" note that they also changed "Rubber Legs" into one word.

But a look at the publishing dates of these various sources shows a trend: The Girdle Bug is becoming the black-rubber-strand version of the white-strand Rubber Legs. Other inconsistencies are also giving way to standards: The rib, underbody, and antennae are disappearing. The only real question that remains unresolved to me is that of distribution of the strands—should they be spaced over the whole shank? or over the front half only? Whole-shank distribution seems to be winning out, but front-half distribution makes the Girdle Bug a fine stonefly-nymph imitation. I'll give you a look at both—you decide.

The Girdle Bug is nearly always weighted and fished well down in streams (sounds suspiciously like a stonefly nymph, doesn't it?). I have no idea who created the Girdle Bug, but if I did, I'd have a lot of questions for him.

GIRDLE BUG

HOOK: Heavy wire, long shank, sizes 10 to 2 (the hook
    shown is an Orvis 1526).
THREAD: Black 3/0.
WEIGHT: Lead wire.
TAILS: Black rubber strands (I prefer the finest diameter).
LEGS: Black rubber strands, three sets (I prefer medium- to
    large diameter).
BODY: Black chenille.

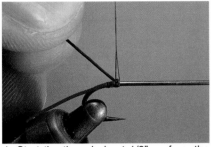

1. Start the thread about 1/8" up from the bend. Wrap it back to the bend and tie in one end of a short length of rubber strand on one side of the shank using a sort of pinch on its side. Wrap the thread forward over the shank and rubber about 1/8", and then draw the forward end of the rubber strand back along the other side of the shank and wrap the thread down it, and the shank, to the bend. Draw both the tail strands together and trim them to length with a single snip.

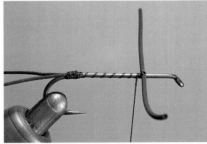

2. Spiral the thread up three-quarters of the shank. There, tie in a 1 1/2" to 2" rubber strand. Use the pinch to secure the strand in line with the shank; then pull the ends of the strand out to a right angle to the shank and secure it in this position with crisscrossing turns of thread.

Tying In Rubber-Strand Legs

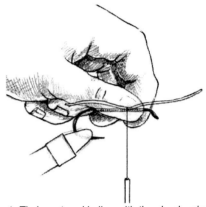

1. Tie in a strand in line with the shank using the pinch.

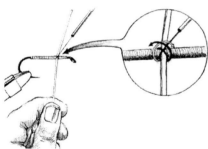

2. Tug the ends of the strand out to the sides, and crisscross the thread over the strand and shank at their juncture. This will set the strand legs permanently into position.

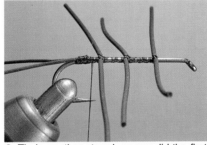

3. Tie in another strand, as you did the first, at midshank. Then tie in another, one-quarter of the shank up from the bend.

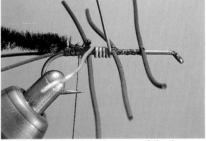

4. From the bend to the rear of the last set of strand-legs, tie in the chenille. Wrap a layer of lead from the front of the last strand legs to just behind the center strand legs.

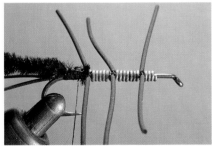

5. Make an open spiral of lead froward one-half turn to the front of the strands—the idea is to keep wrapping without kicking the strands out of position. Continue wrapping the lead in this manner to about 1/8" behind the eye. Trim the lead's ends.

6. If you wish to thicken the thorax and increase weight, use a thicker lead for the front half of the shank than for the rear half. Another approach (shown) is to wrap a second layer of lead from midshank to just short of the end of the first layer. In any case, spiral the thread tightly up the lead to 1/16" behind the eye.

7. Wrap the chenille forward, taking care to preserve the strands' position. Secure the chenille behind the eye with thread turns, trim the chenille closely, build, whip finish, and then trim the thread end to form a thread head.

8. Draw up and trim with a single snip each set of strands; the strand legs should be a shank's length or a bit less.

9. A Girdle Bug with the legs distributed over the front half of the shank only. Tied this way, it bears a strong resemblance to a real stonefly nymph. Trout seem to share this point of view. Note also that a finer chenille was used.

The Red Fox Squirrel Hair Nymph

Long name for a simple nymph, but Dave Whitlock is well known as a keen nymph fisher, so his namesake fly must be taken seriously. Because the Red Fox Squirrel Hair Nymph resembles a lot of aquatic insects without imitating any in particular, it is a true attractor fly.

I first saw the Red Fox Squirrel Hair Nymph—then called the *Dave's* Red-Fox Squirrel Hair Nymph—in *The Masters On The Nymph*, published in 1979. In *The Art of the Trout Fly*, published in 1988, Dave described a different Red Fox Squirrel Hair Nymph; it had gotten simpler. Gone were the swiss-straw wing case and partridge hackle (and "Dave's" and a hyphen). Dave now recommends the one or two turns of dark partridge (or hen saddle) only for the largest hook sizes.

Blending the red-fox squirrel hair and antron for the abdomen can be accomplished in a fur blender or by hand blending. If you are trimming the back fur from the pelt for blending, be sure to leave a patch of fur on the hide for tails. To my knowledge, Dave's use of both squirrel belly and back fur in a single fly is unique. This hair gives the Red Fox Squirrel Hair Nymph its unusual red-and-brown appearance, and is perhaps part of its effectiveness.

Dave includes a layer of lead in his pattern for this fly, but you can tie the Dave's Squirrel Hair Nymph with more lead than this, less, or none at all. Fish the Dave's Squirrel Hair Nymph deep or shallow, dead drift or with imparted motion.

RED FOX SQUIRREL HAIR NYMPH

HOOK: Heavy wire, 2X or 3X long, sizes 18 to 2 (the hook shown is a Mustad 9671).
THREAD: Black 6/0 or 8/0 (for the largest hooks, 3/0 would be good).
WEIGHT: Lead wire.
TAIL: Red-fox-squirrel back guard hair and underfur.
RIB: Fine oval gold tinsel.
ABDOMEN: A blend of one part red-fox-squirrel belly fur and one part a similar shade of antron dubbing (or orlon).
THORAX: Red-fox-squirrel back guard hair and underfur.

1. Add lead, and thread secure it as usual if you want a weighted fly. Snip a tuft of guard hair and fur from the back portion of a red-fox-squirrel pelt. Tie in the tuft at the bend as a tail.

2. Tie in the gold tinsel at the bend. Dub a tapered abdomen up two-thirds of the shank.

3. Wind the tinsel up the abdomen in five to seven ribs. Secure the tinsel's end with thread, and trim the tinsel.

4. Dub a rough, full thorax of guard hair and fur from a red-fox squirrel's back. Form and complete the usual thread head.

5. Here is a Red Fox Squirrel Hair Nymph with one turn of partridge added at the front of the thorax. To make Dave's optional dubbed head, lay a loop of fine leader material over the thread head and secure the loop with two or three thread turns. The loop should project off the eye.

6. Add some head cement—Dave's Flexament, epoxy, whatever—to a couple of inches of thread; add the head cement sparingly.

7. Wrap the thread to the eye and back again to the front of the thorax; all wraps are over the leader loop. Spin some back guard hairs and fur onto the thread and dub to the eye.

8. Cut the thread, put the cut end through the leader loop, and pull the butt of the loop drawing the thread back through and out the back of the head. Trim the thread closely. The end of the thread is whip finished and cemented *under* the dubbed head.

The Bird's Nest

A few months ago, at one of my fly-tying clinics, I was asked to demonstrate the tying of the Bird's Nest. I had to confess that I was unfamiliar with the fly, though I'd heard mention of it. Since then, I've been hearing a lot about the Bird's Nest. One client-friend called last month and told me that he fished the Bird's Nest "all the time." "It almost always gets strikes," he added. "Everyone around here is hot on it." "Here" meant California, but it seems that now anglers everywhere are "hot on it." The sudden popularity of the Bird's Nest seems ironic since Cal Bird, the creator of the Bird's Nest,

tells me that he has been tying and fishing it since 1959.

In describing the tying of the Bird's Nest, Cal simply said that he adds the hackle by "several different methods," so I chose the method that I feel allows the greatest flexibility. The Bird's Nest can also be tied in other colors—cream, olive, and brown—and it can be weighted or unweighted.

The Bird's Nest is another attractor nymph; it suggests no more than a living, edible insect. Fish it dead drift, or try other approaches.

BIRD'S NEST

HOOK: Heavy wire, 1X or 2X long, sizes 16 to 8 (the hook shown is a Daiichi 1710).
THREAD: Tan 8/0 or 6/0.
WEIGHT: Lead wire (optional).
TAIL: Mallard- or teal-flank-feather fibers dyed bronze (or natural bronze mallard).
RIB: Small copper wire.
ABDOMEN: Natural grayish-tan Australian opossum or "Buggy Nymph" dubbing #16.
HACKLE: Mallard- or teal-flank-feather fibers dyed bronze.
THORAX: Same as abdomen.

1. If you want to add lead, do so and secure the lead under thread; if not, start the thread two-thirds up the shank, tie in a section of fibers as a tail (long; about three-quarter shank length). Trim off the fibers' butts. Tie in the copper wire at the bend.

2. Dub a slightly tapered abdomen up two-thirds of the shank. Rib the abdomen with five or six turns of the copper wire. Secure the wire's end with thread, and trim the wire. Add a few extra turns of thread and then add a half hitch.

3. If the fibers of your teal or mallard feather aren't squared at their tips, draw them to whatever angle to the stem will square them. Strip off, or snip off, the section. Hold the section flat over the shank as shown. The tips should reach to the far edge of the hook's bend.

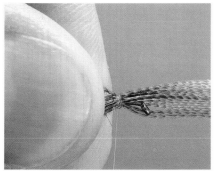

4. With your thumb and finger, roll the fibers around the shank and then press the fibers tight to the abdomen. Take a loose turn of thread around the fibers, and then pull the thread tight. Add a few tight thread turns. Trim the fibers' butts.

5. Build a thorax over the front third of the shank. Build and complete a thread head to complete the Bird's Nest.

The Prince Nymph

The Prince Nymph looks something like a mayfly nymph—a mayfly nymph with two long horns. Since the only place anyone has actually seen a live white-horned mayfly nymph was in a nightmare fueled by a late-night pizza, I put the Prince Nymph in this section rather than in the mayfly section; besides, it looks something like a stone-fly nymph too. But success is the true measure of any fly—the Prince Nymph is a favorite among nymph fishers, and such status tells of success. Perhaps the effectiveness of the Prince Nymph lies in its blend of the familiar and the unusual—a familiar mayfly shape with unusual horns to attract the trout's curiosity. Who really knows?

I have seen this pattern list ostrich herl, peacock herl, and chenille for the body, and I've tied it with each; each looks good. But to demonstrate, I'll use ostrich, as it seems to have been the original. Other variations include brown tails, brown hackle, oval-gold-tinsel rib. The Prince Nymph is sometimes called the Black Forked Tail, but sometimes it is called the Brown Forked Tail, even though the Brown Forked Tail is supposed to be a Prince Nymph variation with a peacock-herl body in place of the usual ostrich, but since the Prince is sometimes tied with peacock, that lets "Brown Forked Tail" jump from variation to simply an alternate title—you see how these things work? Some patterns are laid out plainly in print right from the start; others are passed around, and even modified by their originators over time so that in the end, no one's too sure just what's going on—that is likely the case with the Prince Nymph (or Brown Forked Tail, or whatever). But I forgive fly designers for improving their patterns; it is the natural by-product of a healthy, inquiring spirit.

The Prince Nymph was created by Doug Prince. Fish it as you would any attractor nymph.

PRINCE NYMPH

HOOK: Heavy wire, 2X long, sizes 14 to 6 (the hook shown is an Orvis 1642).
THREAD: Black 8/0 or 6/0.
WEIGHT: Lead wire (optional).
TAIL: Black goose quills.
RIB: Fine oval silver tinsel.
BODY: Black ostrich herl.
HACKLE: Black hen neck hackle.
HORNS: White goose biots.

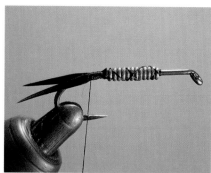

1. If you plan to add lead, do so now. Tie in two goose biots at the bend, curving away from one another. Trim the butts of the biots, or bind their butts under thread.

2. Tie in the tinsel and then three to six (depending on hook size) ostrich herls at the bend. I prefer to tie in the herls just up from their points.

3. If you added lead, taper its ends with dubbing. Advance the thread to about 1/8" behind the eye. Wind the herls forward as a single bunch; slight twisting can help control them. Secure the herls under thread and trim their butts closely.

4. Wind the tinsel up the herl body in six to ten ribs. Secure the tinsel under thread, and trim.

5. Tie in one biot atop the hook so that it projects slightly to the side and reaches back to the bend. Tie in another biot, same length, projecting to the other side. The biots' curves should be up. Trim the biots' butts closely.

6. Prepare and tie in the hackle. Wrap it forward two or three turns, secure its tip under thread, trim the tip, build and complete a thread head. Actually, I prefer to wrap the hackle in the manner described under "The Leadwing Coachman."

The Zug Bug

Like its cousins—the Prince Nymph, Bird's Nest, Red Fox Squirrel Hair Nymph, and others—the Zug Bug bears no special resemblance to a particular insect, but catches a lot of trout.

Cliff Zug created the Zug Bug. Tie it weighted or unweighted, and fish it in all the standard nymph places with all the standard techniques.

ZUG BUG

HOOK: Heavy wire, 1X or 2X long, sizes 14 to 10 (the hook
  shown is a Mustad 9671).
THREAD: Black 8/0 or 6/0.
TAIL: 3 to 6 peacock-sword fibers.
WEIGHT: Lead wire (optional).
RIB: Fine, oval silver tinsel.
BODY: Peacock herl.
HACKLE: Brown hen-neck.
WING CASE: Mallard-flank feather tip, dyed to wood-duck
  color.

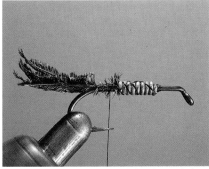

1. Start the thread at midshank, and then spiral it to the bend. Trim off a few peacock sword fibers, and tie them in as a tail. You can use eyed feather herls for the tails, but the sword herls are best. Spiral the thread up about three-quarters of the shank, lower the butts of the fibers, secure them with tight thread turns, and trim the butts closely.

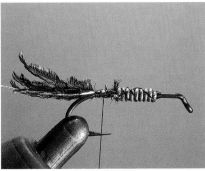

2. If you want to add lead, do so now; then bind it with thread, and taper its ends with dubbing. Tie in the tinsel—hold it sightly above the shank as you spiral the thread down both to the bend. Trim the front of the tinsel, if necessary.

3. Tie in a few herls at the bend. Spiral the thread forward to about 1/8" behind the eye. Wrap the herls forward as one to just behind the eye.

4. Spiral the tinsel up the body as a rib. Thread secure the tinsel just behind the eye, and then trim the tinsel closely.

5. Tie in a hackle just behind the eye. Work the thread back a few turns, and trim the hackle's stem. Wrap the hackle back in two to four turns.

6. Take a couple of thread turns over the hackle's tip; then spiral the thread forward through the fibers. Trim out the hackle's tip. Stroke back the fibers firmly.

Trim the tip out of a mallard-flank feather dyed to wood-duck color. Trim the feather straight across, and then tie it in flat as a wing case extending back about one-third over the body (you can, instead, trim the wing case *after* it is mounted if you like). Build and complete the usual thread head.

The Scud

Fittingly, this trout fly imitates a slow-to-still-water crustacean which most anglers call a scud. A scud is essentially a freshwater shrimp. Imitations of similar pattern—some nearly identical—seem to pop up everywhere. The most common theme for scud imitations is the plastic-strip back. This back, with a rib, convincingly creates the segmented, gelatinous look of a real scud. Randall Kaufmann's *American Nymph Fly Tying Manual* published in 1975 describes Randall's Trout Shrimp, a ribbed plastic-strip scud pattern. Telly Hellekson's *Popular Fly Patterns*, published in 1977 lists an Al Troth pattern, simply called Scud, which also features a ribbed plastic-strip back. Another pattern titled Scud comes from Fred Arbona—can you guess what is its main feature?

These are all good scud imitations. Some tiers follow their patterns faithfully; others take the general idea and do what they want. Al Troth's Scud seems to be as close as any to the fly most often tied for this purpose, and the pattern listed below is very close to Al's ver-

sion. Dave Hughes wrote, "it would be honest for me to confess that when I tie this fly I usually omit the tail, legs, and antennae. The body fur, when picked out, does a fine job of representing the various appendages of the natural." The pattern Dave referred to includes a palmered hackle; other than that, he was referring to almost exactly the pattern I've listed. Dave has eloquently stated my own sentiments concerning tails, legs, and antennae on scud imitations .

Note that the hook described for the Scud is of the English-bait or humped design; this is a good use for such hooks, because scuds themselves are naturally humped. But it is significant that scuds straighten out when they swim, so it is worth considering a conventional hook for a Scud that will be swum.

Scuds (live scuds) are found in still waters and slow-moving streams. Those streams that emerge as tail waters from dams tend to be the ones with the most scuds. If there is some current, you can fish the Scud dead drift; if not, make it swim.

SCUD

> *HOOK*: Heavy wire, English bait or humped design, sizes 16 to 10 (the hook shown is a Dai-Riki 135).
> *THREAD*: 8/0 or 6/0 in a color to match the body.
> *WEIGHT*: Lead wire (optional).
> *TAIL*: Hackle fibers to match the body color (optional).
> *RIB*: Fine, clear monofilament (light tippet is good).
> *BACK*: Clear plastic.
> *BODY*: Natural fur with guard hairs or coarse synthetic dubbing—muskrat, hare's mask, squirrel, australian opossum—in olive or gray or orange or brown or cream or combinations of these colors; the most common color seems to be olive-gray.
> *ANTENNAE*: Hackle fibers to match the body color (optional).

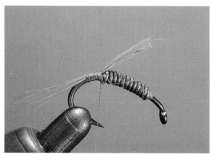

1. If you want to add lead, do so as usual; otherwise, start the thread at midshank, and spiral it to the bend (or down the bend a bit). Weighted or not, use the pinch to tie in a few hackle fibers as a tail. Snip the fibers' butts, or advance the thread and then use the pinch to secure the butts. You can also do what Dave Hughes and I do: Skip the tail altogether.

2. Use the pinch to tie in some fine monofilament at the bend. Cut a strip of plastic sheeting (from a sandwich bag or the like); the strip should be about as wide as the hook's gape. Tie the strip in at the bend; the strip should be flatly horizontal.

3. Dub a thick tapered body to just behind the eye. Pull the plastic strip tightly forward over the top of the body. Secure the strip as you would a wing case. Pull the plastic tight and trim it closely.

4. Wrap the monofilament up the body and plastic in six to eight ribs. Secure the monofilament and trim it just behind the eye.

5. Use the reverse pinch to tie in a few hackle fibers as antennae. Trim the fibers' butts, build a thread head, whip finish the thread, and trim the thread. Pick out some of the hairs and fur from the fly's underside, unless the underside is rough enough without picking. Add head cement to the thread head.

The Bead Head

Some fly tiers take bead-head nymphs as an affront to trout, but trout seem to take bead heads regardless. It *is* disheartening to struggle towards a convincing nymph imitation, one that truly resembles the natural and mimics its movement, only to see the angler next to you clean up using nymphs tied with bulging, gold heads. What makes it worse is that even though dark beads, which *could* create a plausible insect head, are available, the shiny gold beads are the hit with anglers. The day that bead heads make sense, duck hunters will be cutting off the heads of their decoys and replacing them with Christmas-tree ornaments.

But trout seem to take bead heads regardless.

If you can live with bead heads, you'll find that they sink quickly and are simple enough to tie. Most nymph patterns can become bead heads; whether or not they should I leave to you. I have seen two approaches to labeling bead-head nymphs; take the Prince Nymph: It could be the "Bead Head Prince Nymph" or the "GB Prince Nymph." The "GB" stands for "Gold Bead," and this approach makes sense to me, since other bead colors are available.

If you try bead-head nymphs, catch fish on them, and add them to your standard fly selection, I wouldn't spread it around.

1. The bead head has a hole through its center which is small on one side and larger on the other. Slip the small opening over the hook's point, and then slide the bead on up to the eye.

2. Start the thread just behind the bead, and then build dubbing right behind the bead. The dubbing should secure the bead against the eye. Use dubbing of a color that will blend with the front of the fly.

3. Tie the fly as usual. Build a slim thread collar against the rear of the bead, whip finish and trim the thread, add head cement to the thread collar. Fish the completed bead-head nymph when no one else is looking.

IX

BASIC TECHNIQUES

Blending Fur

The various methods for blending fur, and the tools that can be used for it, are described in "Blender" section XI, "Nymph Tying Tools."

Beard Hackle

This is a common feature on nymphs, and it is not really a hackle at all, at least in the stem-wound conventional sense. Inverting the hook can make this procedure easier.

1. Square the tips of the beard fibers, and then strip the fibers from the stem. Hold the fibers beneath the shank, take a turn or two of thread, hold the fibers in place as you tighten the thread.

2. Trim the fibers' butts and proceed.

Breaking the Thread's End

This technique was shown to me by Dan Byford, creator of a popular, tiny-fish imitation called the Zonker. When you first start the thread, make a few turns in one place, keep the thread taut between the bobbin and hook, pull the end of the thread sharply forward, and the thread will break right against the hook. This saves time since you won't have to bother with scissors.

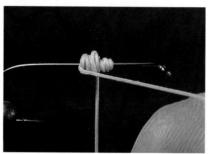

Pull the thread end sharply forward (for clarity, fly-line backing is shown).

Broken Thread

Every tier accidentally breaks thread now and then. Here is the best solution I have found: Clamp hackle pliers to the remaining end of the thread, let the pliers hang, pull some thread from the bobbin, start the thread anew, wrap the new thread back over the end of the old, trim both the new and old thread ends, and continue tying.

With hackle pliers hanging from the broken thread end, start the thread anew over the last turns of the broken thread, and then trim both the new and old thread ends.

Divided Beard Hackle

Like the beard hackle, the divided beard hackle is also not a hackle in the conventional sense.

1. Tie in the leg fibers projecting off the eye. (This can be done early in the tying or late, and sometimes these fibers are the tips of the wing-case fibers.)

2. Pull a bunch of fibers out and then back along one side of the shank and secure them with thread turns.

3. Pull a bunch back along the other side and secure these too. Trim out any remaining fibers and proceed.

4. A completed divided beard hackle.

Dubbing

The common, simplest approach to dubbing is described in section I, "Essential Techniques." Shown here are two alternate methods. First is a method that results in tightly wound fibers and a slim body.

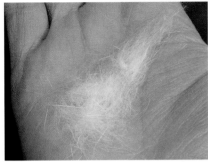

1. Lay dubbing fibers in the palm of your hand and tease them into a roughly triangular shape.

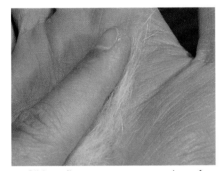

2. Slide a finger across your palm a few times to roll the fibers into a tapered rope, and then trim the rope's very tip to eliminate fuzz.

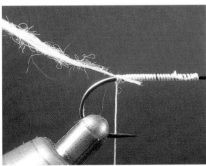

3. Using the pinch (or a light turn) Secure the fine tip of the rope under a turn or two of thread.

4. Spin the thread and the large end of the rope together, and then hold the end of the rope-thread combination as you wind it up the shank.

This final dubbing method—the dubbing loop—can create a scruffy effect, a bulky one, or a trim, tight one all depending on how you handle it. The benefits of a dubbing loop are that it secures the dubbing especially well and that it allows for quick bulk and a rough-but-secure effect. The loop is formed by pulling some extra thread off the bobbin, looping it over a dubbing twister (or even your finger), and then wrapping the thread around the shank again and wrapping back far enough to lock in the ends of the loop. For the scruffy effect, hook a dubbing twister (or simply a half-straightened paper clip) onto the loop, distribute fur inside the loop, twist the loop, and wrap the thread-fur combination up the shank.

1. Distribute the fur inside the loop.

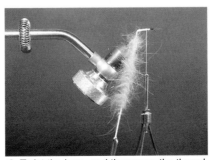

2. Twist the loop, and then wrap the thread-fur combination up the shank.

A variation of the dubbing-loop method involves spinning the dubbing onto the thread, doubling the thread into a loop, and then spinning the loop as before. Dubbing lightly applied will really lie down; applied heavily and roughly it will provide bulk, and the dubbing will still smooth out well.

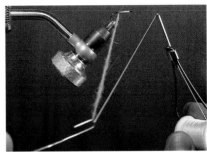

1. Spin the dubbing onto the thread as usual. With the twisting tool hooked in the thread, double the thread and secure its end with thread turns to form a loop.

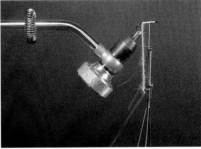

2. Twist the loop and wrap it up the shank.

Dubbing-Loop Collar

This is a fine way to create a collar of just about any fiber—fur, hair, feather fibers, or whatever will spin in a dubbing loop. Waxing the thread can help control the fibers.

1. Wax the thread, and then double it and secure its ends under thread turns. Distribute the fibers along the loop, all tips on one side, all butts on the other. Keep the butts short. Pinch the sides of the loop together to hold the fibers.

2. Slip some kind of dubbing twister into the end of the loop and spin the twister and loop.

3. Moisten the fibers and stroke the long tips to one side of the loop.

4. Advance the thread, wrap the loop forward in close consecutive turns, stroke back the fibers after each turn. Secure the end of the loop under tight thread turns, trim the loop's end.

5. A completed dubbing-loop colar.

Flat-Feather Legs

I particularly like this method of creating nymph legs. It is described in detail under "Morristones and Quiverstones." Flat-feather legs can incorporate all kinds of feathers—hen saddle, hen neck, partridge flank, various pheasant-body feathers to name a few. And a nymph needn't be as big as a Morristone to use flat-feather legs; all kinds of mayfly nymphs use them, even on some small hooks.

Lead

In order to get nymphs well down in moving water, lead of one form or another is often a necessity. (In lakes, flies are usually sent down on sinking lines.) Lead can be added directly to the leader, and often this is the only practical way to get a nymph—even a heavily weighted nymph—down in swift currents. But using lead in the tying of nymphs is the most common way to make them sink.

Lead comes in several sizes, and fly shops use different descriptions for those sizes—one shop's "fine" lead may be another's "#1" lead and so on. The point is, the finer leads are usually used for tiny hooks, the medium-size leads are for medium-size hooks, and the largest leads are for big hooks. Because most nymphs are tied on a wide range of hook sizes, and because different sources use different designations for lead sizes, it is difficult to suggest a lead size in a pattern, but the photos should help clarify.

Lead is wrapped, in close turns, over a spiraled-thread base, and then the lead is secured with tight thread-wrappings. I build tight turns of thread behind the lead, spiral the thread at a steep angle up to the lead's front (a steep angle keeps the thread from stalling in the slots between turns of lead), and then add tight turns at the lead's front—the tight turns of thread keep the lead from later spreading out. From here I spiral the thread to wherever the actual tying of the fly begins.

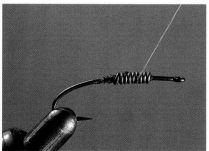

1. After adding tight thread turns at the lead's rear, spiral the thread forward at a steep angle.

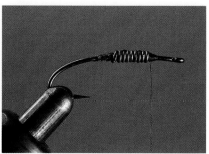

2. Add tight thread turns at the lead's front.

A second layer of lead can be added over the first for a very heavy fly, but it is important to consider how this thick foundation will affect the form of the finished fly—additional lead on the leader may be a better answer than an unnaturally plump mayfly nymph. If you do decide to add a second layer of lead, keep its ends well inside the ends of the first layer. This way, there will be at least some graduation of diameter rather than a sheer two-layer dropoff to climb materials up and down. The second layer of lead shouldn't be too tight; otherwise it will spread out the first layer.

Once lead is wrapped onto a hook, you will need to trim its ends. I used to cut the lead's ends with old scissors or deep into the blades of a good pair (to protect the sharpness of the fine points), until I found out about breaking lead. As my friend John Smeraglio was tying a batch of Deschutes Cased Caddises one morning at his fly shop on the Deschutes River, I saw how easily he broke off the ends of his lead. He left the lead on the spool, held one end close to the shank, wrapped the other end up the shank, and then pulled the ends until they broke cleanly. "Just press your thumbnail into the lead as you pull," he said."The lead will stretch a little, and then break neatly right against the shank." He was right; it's a great way to remove the ends. If the ends stick out at all, you can press them down easily with a fingernail or thumbnail. If your materials resist the jump from shank to lead, add a bit of dubbing at the ends of the lead to taper the transition; the extra second or two this requires may speed up the tying that follows and make for a better-looking fly.

On stream, it is common to see anglers tossing nymphs in the air and catching them in open palms, like a spiritless attempt at juggling. These anglers are trying to guess how heavily their nymphs are weighted. You can avoid the juggling syndrome by using different thread colors for different amounts of lead. I like to use pale thread for unweighted nymphs, black for moderately weighted, and red for heavily weighted. I saw this idea in print in an issue of *Flyfishing* magazine. It works. And head cement makes the red heads subdued enough to satisfy me and the fish. For details of adding lead to both standard nymphs and big nymphs, see these sections: "The Gold Ribbed Hare's Ear and Weighting Most Nymphs" and "The Box Canyon Stone and Weighting Big Nymphs."

Measuring

As a general rule, materials are measured against the length of a hook, but occasionally they are measured against a hook's gape. Hackles are used more in dry flies than nymphs, but a dry-fly hackle gauge can be helpful in sizing hen hackles, body feathers, and such for nymphs and soft-hackle flies.

In general, these are the proportions I use for nymphs: Tails are half to two-thirds the length of the shank; the abdomen reaches to just past midshank; and the wing case starts just ahead of midshank and stops about 1/16″ behind the eye (the 1/16″ is for the thread head); legs (or whatever represents them) are measured by the same guidelines as are tails. Be prepared, however, to discard these proportions for specific patterns—caddis pupae, and their imitations, have long abdomens and short thoraxes, and soft-hackle flies have leg-suggesting fibers that some tiers make fully as long as the entire hook, and there are lots of other fly patterns that break my rules.

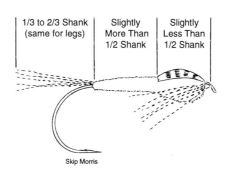

Skip Morris

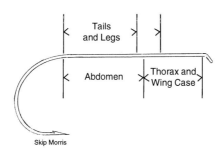

Skip Morris

The best way I've found to mark a measured point on a material is to hold the material in such a way that the measured point is seen by sighting along the edge or tip of the thumb. Another method is to note the measured point and keep an eye on it until the material is positioned and secured. Some materials, such as barred hackle-tips and fibers, have markings that can be used to identify a measured point.

Note that the edge of the thumb marks the measured tie-in point.

After a material is tied in, you can use the tips of your scissors, as you would a draftsman's compass, to check the length of the material against the hook—simply open the blades until the distance between their tips is equal to the distance measured; hold the scissors firmly at their joint to secure the tips' position.

Using scissor tips to check measurements.

The One-Handed Whip Finish

Eventually you will probably want to learn the one-handed whip finish, as it is quickest. Start with a half hitch. With the half-hitch loop held above the hook by your first and second fingers, turn your hand so it is palm down. Pull one side of the loop forward with your second finger. Swing the loop's side around until it and the tip of your second finger are on the near side of the hook. At this point your hand and fingers should be above the hook with the tip of your first finger on the far side of the hook and the tip of your second finger on the hook's near side. Now lower your hand, and the loop, below the hook. That's one whip-finish turn completed.

Swing the loop towards you and then above the hook again. With your palm down, repeat the previous sequence to add another whip-finish turn. When you have enough turns in place (three is about right), close the loop with a pointed object as already described.

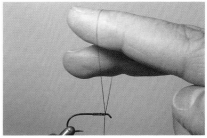

1. With a half-hitch loop formed, rotate your palm down. Then draw your second finger's tip, and that side of the loop, to the near side of the hook.

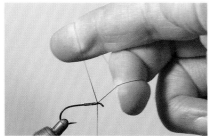

2. With your first finger guiding its side of the loop to the far side of the hook, lower your hand to complete that turn.

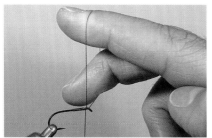

3. Swing the loop again over the hook, and with your palm down repeat the sequence.

The One Handed Whip Finish

1. Rotate your hand within the half hitch loop. Your palm should face down. Hook your second finger back.

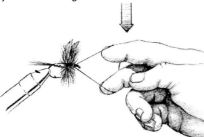

2. Lower your hand with the tip of your first finger on the far side of the hook and the tip of your second finger on the near side.

3. Swing the loop up the near side of the hook. When your hand is over the hook again, add another turn to the whip finish exactly as before.

Palmering Hackle

"Palmered" hackle is hackle that has been wound in open spirals; "palmering" hackle is the act of winding it in open spirals.

The simplest way to palmer a hackle is to prepare the hackle, tie it in by its stem, and wind it forward with hackle pliers. Easy.

Palmering a hackle by its tip.

This next method creates a taper of fibers from short at the rear to longer at the front. Draw the fibers back from the sides of a hackle, exposing its tip. Tie in the tip. Wind the hackle forward by its butt. The tricky part here is to get the hackle started. As you first begin to wrap the hackle, reach in with your bodkin or scissors' tips and tease any wild fibers back into their natural direction, sweeping back towards the hackle's tip. Once this is under control, the hackle will usually wrap neatly.

Hackle pliers can usually be omitted with this method.

1. Stroke back the fibers from a hackle's tip in preparation for palmering.

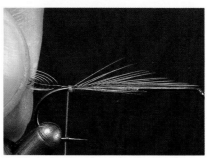

2. Tie in the hackle by its tip. Create the body that the hackle will be palmered over.

3. Tease any wild hackle fibers back as you start winding the hackle.

4. Palmer the hackle by its butt.

The final method for palmering a hackle was established when the Elk Hair Caddis, a floating caddis imitation developed by Al Troth, became popular. It is a method used primarily on dry flies, but it suits nymphs, and I feel certain we will see its use increase in nymph patterns. Al's method slants the hackle fibers back, makes palmering a hackle with its tip toward the bend easy, and reinforces the hackle and whatever is under it with turns of wire—all desirable features at times. For details on this method, see "The Woolly Bugger and an Exercise in Tying Efficiency."

1. With wire (copper, silver, or gold) tied in at the bend and the hackle tied in up the shank, palmer the hackle back to the bend.

2. Hold the hackle pliers up and back (or let the pliers hang) and take a turn of wire over the hackle's tip. Add one more turn of wire at the bend, rib the wire forward through the hackle, and secure the wire with thread turns.

Reinforcing Peacock Herl

Fragile peacock herl is usually protected by ribbing or a palmered hackle, but without these it can be reinforced by twisting it around the working thread. Simply tie in the herl, and then spin it and the thread in one direction between your thumbs and fingers of both hands. The twisted thread and herl will soon look almost like chenille. If the herl's quill is too wide to spin easily, bring the bobbin close and hold the herl against the bobbin's tube and spin both.

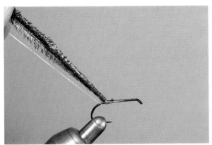

1.Tie in the herl and hold it along the thread.

2. Spin both together.

3. Hold the thread and the end of the herl as you wrap them as one up the shank.

The Reverse Pinch

The reverse pinch is merely a pinch performed with the other hand, the hand projecting off the hook's eye rather than cupped over the hook's shank and bend as usual. In other words—switch hands and switch sides of the pinch loop and you've turned the pinch into the reverse pinch. The reverse pinch is sometimes used to protect fragile materials, and other times because the conventional pinch just won't work.

1. The reverse pinch is executed in exactly The same manner as is the standard pinch; the only change is in which hand holds the material.

2. The results of a properly executed reverse pinch.

Shaping Spun Hair

In most cases, the first cut in spun hair should be along the underside of the shank. Secure the hook by its bend in a pair of pliers, old fly-tying vise jaws, midge vise jaws, or the like (you can hold the hook in your fingers, but

it's awkward and a bit dangerous). Sight down the front of the hook and saw a razor blade along the shank's underside, *but be careful not to cut so close that you nick the thread.* Do this in more than one attempt if you fear nicking the thread—the first cut will give you a clearer view. Try to avoid touching the blade to the hook's bend, as this will quickly dull the blade.

Turn the hook upside down, decide how you want to shape the hair, and make a razor cut on each side. Do the same along the top of the hair. You now have the hair cut to its basic dimensions with a square cross section. Round the hair with razor strokes.

Of course you can do all this with scissors, but I think the razor blade is easiest. Double-edged safety blades work, but injector and double-edged blades are sharper. I like to split double-edged blades in half for safety, this can be done with tin snips.

1. Make the first cut along the hook's underside.

2. Make the side cuts with the hook inverted.

3. Make the top cut.

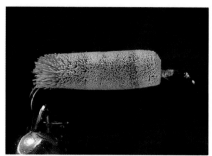

4. Trim the front and rear of the body a bit, and then round out the edges.

Spinning Deer Hair

Spun hair is commonly used on dry flies and bass bugs. The hairs that spin best—deer, elk, and caribou—are filled with tiny air pockets and this gives them buoyancy. But spun hair can add lots of bulk, which is sometimes desireable in nymphs. Besides, now that nymphs are often fished near, in, and even on the surface, spun deer will probably show up in more and more nymph patterns.

To spin deer, elk, or caribou hair, begin with size-A rod winding thread secured to the shank. Ahead of the thread should be only bare shank. Snip a small batch of hair close to the hide (usually the bunch is about the diameter of a pencil, but this will vary with hook size). Hold the hair bunch firmly by its tips and stroke the fuzz from it with any comb. Snip the tips from the hair bunch. Hold the hair to the shank with one end down and towards the hook's eye and the other end of the hair up and slanting back; the hair should be on the near side of the hook.

Take three light turns of thread around the hair and shank. Tighten the thread slowly as you slowly release the hair bit by bit. The hair will spin around the shank and distribute itself as you tighten the thread.

Once the thread is tight, draw back the hair and hold it firmly as you pull the thread tightly forward and take four turns of it against the front of the hair. Prepare and spin on another hair bunch; then support the hair from behind as you push back on the front of the hair, compressing the second bunch back into the first, but keep this in mind: If you want your fly to sink, less compression means less buoyancy. Snip, comb, spin, and compress more hair bunches until the proper amount of shank is covered. Whip finish the thread and trim its end. Remove the hook from your vise and shape the hair.

I tried everything I could think of to make hair spin, but nothing really worked until I discovered that the rate at which the hair is released is just as critical as the rate at which the thread is tightened. Practice towards blending these factors for good spinning. And when you release the hair, don't just loosen your grip on it; *completely* release hairs from the side of the bunch. You should be able to see the ends of the hair springing free of your grasp.

1. Comb a bunch of deer hair.

2. Trim the tips of the hair.

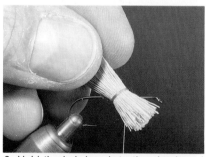

3. Hold the hair bunch to the shank and wrap the thread around it three times. (Orange thread is shown for clarity, but thread color is usually close to hair color.)

4. Gradually tighten the thread as you gradually release the hair—spinning hair.

5. A spun hair bunch.

6. Draw the hair tightly back and the thread tightly forward. Add four tight thread turns in front of the hair.

7. Compress each spun bunch into the last.

Splayed Beard Hackle

To me, this looks more like real nymph legs than the standard beard hackle and can almost always be substituted for it. The technique for executing it is similar to the one described in "The Bird's Nest."

1. Square the tips of a section of feather fibers and strip them from the stem. With the hook inverted, hold the fibers just above the shank in your right hand (right handers); try to keep the section's flats horizontal.

2. Lower your left-hand thumb and first finger down over the section, wrapping the section around half of the shank. Add a tight turn of thread using the pinch. Trim the butts and continue tying.

3. A finished splayed beard hackle.

4. A splayed beard hackle can begin as a wound hackle collar.

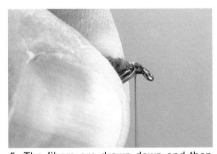

5. The fibers are drawn down and then secured there with thread.

6. A splayed beard hackle from a wound hackle collar.

Split Tails

Split tails are often used on dry flies, seldom on nymphs. But with the increasing interest in imitating partially hatched insects at the surface, dry-fly-style split tails will be showing up on more and more fly patterns loosely categorized as nymphs. Renee' Harrop's floating nymphs were among the first nymphs with split tails. Incidentally, the term "split tails" as we are using it here refers to fibers split around a ball of thread or dubbing. The tails of the Morristone are split, but that's another matter.

Here are three methods for creating split tails; try all three and then decide which you prefer.

The first method is to build a tiny ball of dubbing at the bend, strip two to four fibers from a hackle, tie in the fibers crossways to form one tail bunch, repeat the process to form the other tail bunch, trim or thread bind the fibers butts. A couple of pointers: Use very little dubbing to form the ball as most tiers use far too much, and position the fibers to allow for torque, then they will rotate to their proper place when you tighten the thread.

1. Create a tiny dubbing ball.

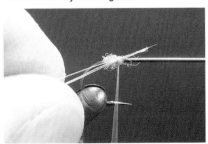

2. Tie in a bunch of fibers on the near side of the hook.

3. Tie in a bunch of fibers on the far side.

I discovered this second method in Dave Whitlock and Robert Boyle's book *The Fly-Tyer's Almanac* in the section about Rene' and Bonnie Harrop. Create a tiny ball of dubbing at the bend again, tie in four to eight hackle fibers up the shank, wrap the thread toward the bend; as the thread nears the dubbing ball divide the fibers into two groups.

1. Tie in hackle fibers (the ball of dubbing has already been formed). Divide the fibers into two groups while winding the thread to the ball.

This third method for creating split tails is my own. For me, it is the fastest. Create a ball of *thread* at the bend; eight to ten thread turns should do it. Crisscross the thread over itself as you build it up. Run the thread up the shank and tie in a bunch of hackle fibers. Wind the thread to within three close turns of the thread ball, and then pull the fibers firmly down against the thread ball so that the fibers tip downwards; some of the fibers will stay atop the ball and others will slip to the sides. Add the last tight turns of thread against the ball; then wrap the thread forward a few turns. Release the fibers. Snip out the fibers in the center leaving a small bunch on either side.

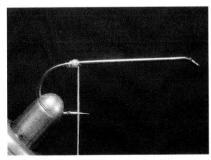

1. Build a thread ball, spiral the thread forward, and tie in the fibers.

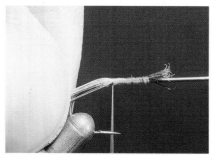

2. Wrap the thread down the fibers and shank towards the ball. As the thread nears the ball, pull the fibers tightly down and wind the thread right against the thread ball. Wrap the thread forward a few turns.

3. Snip out the center fibers leaving a small bunch on each side.

Stacking

The best way to stack hair is with a hair stacker. To do this, simply comb a bunch of hair—deer, caribou, calf tail, buck tail, and others—drop the bunch tip first into the stacker, tap the stacker a few times against a table top, hold the stacker horizontal, remove the stacker's cap, and remove the stacked hair, its tips neatly squared.

Here are a few pointers about stacking hair in a hair stacker: Kinky hair, such as calf tail, stacks best if it is thoroughly combed, end to end. When removing hair from a stacker, grasp the hair by its tips; and doing so deliberately, not with a lot of extra movement, will best keep the tips squared. If your hair bunch is too large, hold it by its butts and remove fibers from the edges of the bunch.

If you are tying several flies with stacked hair, stacking hair for each one can be tedious. I prefer to stack a big bunch of hair, trim the hairs' butts square, fold a piece of masking tape over the butts, and clamp the taped butts in a bulldog clip. Then you can snip a bunch of hairs from either side of the main bunch as needed.

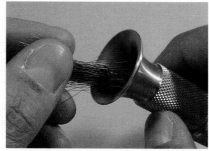

1. Snip and comb a small bunch of hair, and then drop it point first into the stacker.

2. Tap the stacker.

3. Remove the hair with deliberate movements.

4. To keep the tips squared on a large batch of hair, trim the butts square, and then wrap masking tape around the butts.

5. Clamp the butts in a bulldog clip.

Hair can be stacked by hand, though the results will never compare with those of a hair stacker. One way is to snip a large bunch of hair, and then grasp the tips of the very longest hairs and draw those hairs from the bunch. These hairs will be somewhat squared at their tips. You can keep repeating the process taking the next longest hairs and then the next longest and so on.

1. Draw the long fibers from a big hair bunch; these long fibers will be somewhat stacked.

2. The results.

Another method is to draw the long hairs from a small hair bunch, and then lay this bunch alongside the main bunch, tips evened. Repeat this sequence until you are satisfied with the results.

1. Draw the long hairs from a small hair bunch.

2. Lay the new bunch alongside the old, tips squared. Repeat this sequence until you are satisfied with the results.

Tapered Cuts

Almost every time you cut a material on a fly, you will serve yourself well to make that cut tapered. Blunt cuts make tiny shelves that thread wants to slide down, and blunt cuts also make bumps and gaps that create fly bodies with bumps and gaps; tapered cuts make for long, low angles over which thread wraps easily and neatly, and tapered cuts provide smooth foundations for ribs and bodies.

Tapered Cuts

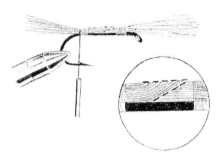

Thread Tension

As a general rule, thread turns should be as tight as possible, to create a durable fly. Dave Hughes, in his book *American Fly Tying Manual*, recommends wrapping thread onto a hook and then breaking it intentionally in order to develop a sense of the thread's strength—good advice. Another way to insure tight thread wraps is to grasp a hook to support it as needed—many hooks are flexible and need this.

Exceptions to the tight-thread rule are common with dry flies, uncommon with nymphs. The point is, watch for exceptions, but when none exist, follow the tight-thread rule.

Wet Whip Finish

Some dry flies and nymphs have a dubbed head, so their thread head needn't suggest the head of an insect; in fact, the thread head here is best kept as tiny as possible, inconspicuous, too tiny to distort or compete with the dubbed head. This is accomplished with no real thread head at all, just a wet whip finish.

The wet whip finish consists of a few thread turns and a whip finish. It's the method of applying the cement that makes it work.

1. With the dubbed-head formed, apply a small amount of cement along one-quarter to one-half inch of thread, near the hook.

2. Add two or more turns of the thread to get some cement onto the hook. With some cemented thread still free, add a whip finish, and trim the thread. The cement is all through the whip finish, and all is secure.

3. A completed wet whip finish—nearly nonexistent.

Wings—Down, Quill

Set two quill sections cupped together with their long sides up (some tiers prefer the long sides down). Measure the quills so that they will extend slightly beyond the far edge of the hook's bend. Hold the cupped sections in place and tie them in using the wing pinch; add a few tight thread turns. Trim the butts of the quills at an angle and bind the trimmed butts under tight thread wraps.

For the best results, tie in the wings one at a time, again using the wing pinch. Just make certain the first wing is firmly mounted before adding the second.

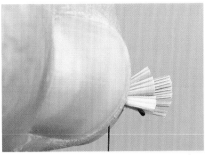

1. Once measured, tie in the wings using the wing pinch; then add several tight securing thread turns.

2. Trim the sections' butts at an angle; bind the trimmed butts under tight thread wraps.

The Wing Pinch

The wing pinch is a variation of the regular pinch. As the pinch loop is tightened, the pinch finger and thumb are slid down slightly to help compress the wing neatly; care is taken to preserve the wings' flatness. Also, it helps to draw the thread not only down but also slightly towards you.

1. As you tighten the loop, slide your finger and thumb slightly down around the shank.

The Wing Pinch

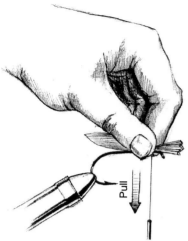

Thumbtip and fingertip slide down slightly around the shank as the pinch loop closes.

Wing–Case Construction

This is the basic method and simple enough: The material is tied in, the thorax is formed, the wing-case material is pulled forward and secured with thread turns. But a few pointers will make wing-case construction easy and fast and will insure neat, flat wing cases.

When you handle the wing-case fibers don't bunch them; rather try to preserve their flatness, and then secure them using the "wing-case pinch," a variation of the pinch in which the flat wing-case material is rolled over the top half of the fly, held fast all around behind the tie-in point by the tips of the thumb and first finger, held in position as the thread is brought over it, and then secured by rolling the tips of the thumb and finger forward over the thread and then pulling the thread tight. Several tight thread turns should be added right away at the tie-in point before proceeding.

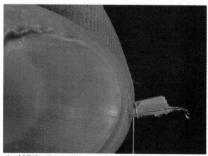

1. With the wing-case fibers rolled flatly over the thorax area, hold them stationary with the tips of your thumb and finger.

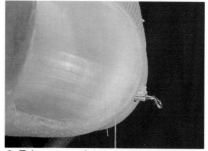

2. Take a turn of thread, roll the tips over the thread turn, and tighten the thread.

When you pull the wing-case material forward, keep it flat, and then keep modest tension (too much tension will make the fibers want to pull free later) on it as you work the bobbin over the front of the material with your other hand. Let the bobbin hang as you reach around and pull it down to tighten the thread. Add a few tight thread turns at the tie-in point and then proceed.

1. Hold the wing-case fibers flat and under modest tension as you work a turn of thread over them and pull it tight.

Wing–Case Pinch

Described under "Wing-Case Construction" just previous to this.

X

NYMPH TYING MATERIALS

In *The Art of Tying the Dry Fly,* I said that, in my opinion, the common denominator among dry-fly materials is buoyancy. Conversely (and predictably), I believe that the common denominator among nymph materials is the inclination to sink.

Of course there are lots of exceptions to both statements. Consider those buoyant or neutral materials that add a certain appropriate sparkle or texture; would they be passed over in favor of a denser material that failed to offer these qualities? Not likely. Take peacock herl—it's been used in dry flies for as long as I can remember for its emerald brilliance, and it's been used in nymphs for just as long for that same brilliance. Peacock herl is more-or-less neutral; that is, it barely floats. So it doesn't really help a dry fly to float or a nymph to sink; it offers something else.

Still, buoyancy, or the lack of it, determines whether most materials are delegated to nymphs or dry flies. Take hackles—rooster-neck hackles are resistant to water, so they usually wind up in dry flies; soft, absorbent hen hackles usually wind up in nymphs. It's all pretty logical: Follow the rules unless there is sufficient reason to break them.

Of course the line between dry flies and nymphs is now blurred as never before. The first nymph in this book, the Fur Nymph, floats. To some, that would make it a dry fly, and that point of view could be well argued. But because the Fur Nymph imitates a true nymph—it lacks even a semblance of wings—I have listed it as a nymph. Such hard-to-categorize fly patterns are common, now that we explore and imitate all kinds of previously ignored insect stages.

So I offer here what I find to be common nymph-tying materials. But keep an open mind, for there are always uncommon possibilities worth exploring.

Lead

There is one purpose only for lead: to add weight. Lead comes in many thicknesses, and different fly shops describe it with different systems—one shop's "#3" lead may be another's "medium." I've found a medium, or slightly smaller than medium, lead to be the most versatile; I can use it in a size-12 Gold Ribbed Hare's Ear or a size-6 Box Canyon Stone. But fine leads are handy for small nymphs, and thick leads for big nymphs. Copper wire is sometimes used to weight nymphs, and it can even be used in place of tying thread as a method of adding weight.

Tinsels and Wires

These have always been, and still are, a common component of nymph patterns. The standard use of tinsels and wires is for ribbing. Tinsels always used to be metal, but mylar is now the standard.

Wires create subtle ribs. Gold and silver wires are fine, but copper wire, which comes in various thicknesses, has a somber appearance even at its thickest.

Oval tinsels have long come in silver and gold, but now they come in all sorts of colors. There are various thicknesses of oval tinsels.

Flat tinsels commonly come in silver and gold, but other colors are surfacing. Particularly handy is flat tinsel that is silver on one side and gold on the other. Flat tinsels range from fine to broad.

Cements

For cementing the thread head of any fly—dry fly, nymph, streamer, whatever—there are lots of good commercial head cements. My favorite, however, is an epoxy glue called Crystal Clear Epoxy, made by the Epoxy Coatings Company and marketed as a rod-builder's glue. Dave's Flexament and Tuffilm (available in art stores) have proved valuable for

Red-Fox Squirrel

Australian Opossum

Otter

Rabbit

Red-Fox Squirrel Tail

Wood Chuck

Muskrat

Red Fox

Beaver

Caribou

Deer

Wood Chuck

Hare's Mask

Moose Body

Elk

Materials

1. Floss
2. Thread
3. Size-A Rod-Winding Thread
4. Copper Wire
5. Lead
6. Gold Wire
7. Oval Silver Tinsel
8. Flat Mylar Tinsel
9. Silver Wire

Brian Rose Photo

toughening wet-fly wings, among other uses.

Threads

For all-around tying of trout flies there is 8/0 and 6/0 thread—I really like 8/0— and for big flies or flies that require lots of thread tension there is 3/0; for flaring and spinning hair I prefer size-A rod-winding thread. There are special tiny-fly threads, but I use 8/0 for even the smallest hooks.

Fly-tying threads are available prewaxed or unwaxed. Prewaxed threads are only lightly waxed and most tiers choose them. Fly-tying wax can be purchased separately and added as needed to either prewaxed or unwaxed threads. A full color range of threads is fun to work with, but I feel that brown and tan are all you really need.

Feathers

Hen-chicken neck and saddle hackles are webby, soft, and absorbent, so they are used frequently in nymphs as tails and legs, whereas rooster-chicken hackles are too stiff and hard for common use in nymphs. Feathers which can be matched for wet-fly wings include body feathers such as turkey flats, wood duck, partridge, grouse, teal, mallard, and mallard and turkey quills; all the body feathers just mentioned also make fine nymph tails. Pheasant-tail fibers are popular for nymph legs and tails. Herls, peacock and ostrich, add fullness to nymphs, and peacock has a special emerald brilliance that nymph tiers and trout both appreciate. Marabou is so soft that it is mostly used in streamer flies, but its properties also find a place in nymphs. *All* of the feathers just described are used to form wing cases.

Furs

Furs used to dub nymphs include badger, muskrat, beaver, mole, red fox, otter, wood-chuck underfur, and versatile dyed and natural squirrel, rabbit, and Australian opossum—these last three have heavy guard hairs that can be picked out to suggest legs (rabbit in the form of hare's mask). Antron is often blended with natural furs to add sparkle.

Yarns

I generally think of yarn as a substitute for dubbing. The idea is, if I need to add bulk or to cover a lot of shank or lead, I consider yarn first—spinning enough dubbing onto thread to handle these situations can be dreadfully slow.

The old standard is wool yarn, but antron yarn offers sparkle (it is also an integral part of the Emergent Sparkle Pupa). Leech yarn is a fuzzy yarn used for creating leech imitations.

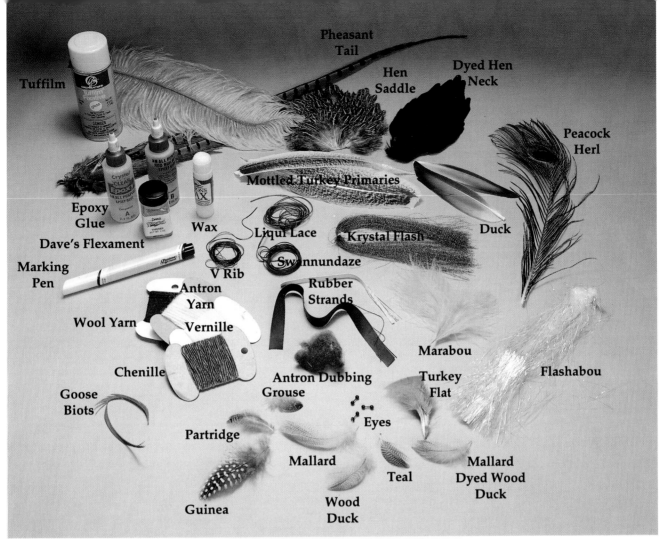

Brian Rose Photo

Hairs

Hair tends to be buoyant, so it is commonly a dry-fly material. But in small quantities, hair's buoyancy is of no consequence, and only hair can do the things that hair can do.

Hairs such as moose and squirrel tail make tough wing cases; these, and the heavy guard hairs of such furs as squirrel body and hare's mask, are sometimes used as nymph tails. The hollow hairs—deer, elk, and caribou—can be spun, flared, and shaped to create bulk, and in a few cases to add buoyancy. Hollow hairs also make buoyant wings which help suspend emerger flies.

Various Materials

Goose and turkey biots are the standard for tails on stonefly-nymph imitations. Biots are sometimes used for ribs and, on small nymphs, for wing cases.

Floss is the old standard for all kinds of floating and sinking flies, and it is still used frequently today. Lots of sparkling synthetic materials are showing up in new nymph patterns. A sample list of such materials includes the following: Krystal Flash, Flashabou, Glitter Body, Frostbite. Some synthetic dubbings offer subdued sparkle; such dubbings may be labeled with a brand name, or by the fiber, such as Antron dubbing. Plastic eyes used to involve short lengths of thick leader material, a flame, a lot of messing around, and a considerable amount of smoke; but now that plastic eyes are premade in several sizes, they are increasingly showing up in nymph patterns, especially big nymph-patterns. Synthetic rib materials such as Swannundaze, Larva Lace, and V rib offer a gelatinous appearance; sometimes these are used not just as a rib but as a body material. Finally, now that rubber strand is available in rounded shapes and finer diameters than before, you will surely see it used more and more as nymph legs and even tails.

Waxes

Fly-tying wax can be soft or hard. Both are good, but I prefer soft. Wax is usually added to thread for a procedure called dubbing.

XI

NYMPH TYING TOOLS

The notion of a complete set of separate tools for tying nymphs, another for dry flies, and so on is silly—nearly all the tools listed here are used for tying all kinds of flies, including nymphs. Nevertheless, the ways in which fly-tying tools are used are sometimes different for nymphs than for other flies. So here is a rundown of fly-tying tools from the nymph-tier's perspective.

Vise

If a fly-tying vise is sturdy, holds a wide range of hooks firmly, opens and tightens easily, and allows plenty of tying access, it is a good vise.

Vises are clamp-mounted or base-mounted. Clamps are more secure, but I like my base-mounted vise because it is portable, and secure enough.

"Rotary" vises allow you to rotate the jaws to inspect a fly and work on it from all sides; "stationary" vises have a set jaw position. I tied with a good stationary vise for many years and it served me honorably—I even tied flies that won competitions on it—but now I'm sold on my rotary vise. I guess that says it: A stationary vise is fine (and usually reasonably priced), but a rotary vise has some advantages that can grow on you.

Scissors

Don't skimp—good scissors are essential. And get scissors made especially for fly tying. I like scissors with finely serrated edges; these edges hold materials in place.

Bobbin

Holds thread and floss and sometimes other materials. It's crazy to even consider tying without a thread bobbin. One is enough, but more are handy.

A floss bobbin is optional, but I use one more and more. Although a thread bobbin will handle floss, the floss bobbin's wide tube with a flared end is best.

Hackle Pliers

These are mostly used for winding hackles on dry flies, but there are plenty of occasions when the tying of a nymph will call for them. As to the many hackle-plier styles—if a pair holds the hackle securely and has a loop for the tier's finger, it's a good pair. Some tiers don't use the finger loop in hackle pliers, so they don't miss it if it's absent. I still prefer the classic rounded-jaw all-metal pliers.

Light

Some kind of adjustable light that will pour lots of light right down on the jaws of your vise is a must. Plenty of ambient light also helps.

Those are the tools you need; I'd be reluctant to tie without them. The next tools are optional but useful.

Optional Tools

Magnifier

For anglers with limited eyesight or eyesight diminished by age, mag-nifiers may well be a requirement. Tying tiny flies may also demand magnification. There are large arm-mounted lenses, some with built-in light, and these work well. Another good option is reading glasses, which are essentially magnifiers. Glasses with magnification of 2.5 may be enough for slightly limited sight and standard-size trout flies; for the same sight and tiny flies, magnification of 3.5 to 4.5 may be required. My current choice in a magnifier is a "binocular magnifier," a headband with a hinged visor in which the visor holds two lenses, the kind of magnifier a jeweler wears. With the binocular visor one can replace the lenses, connected into a single unit called a "lens plate," and vary magnification through a considerable range. The performance of binocular visors is excellent; their hinged visor is handy; they can be worn over glasses; their price is most reasonable. Binocular visors can be purchased at jeweler's supply houses.

A binocular magnifier.

Lamp

HMH Base Vise

Magnifying Glasses

Floss Bobbin

Ceramic Bobbin

Hair Stacker

C-clamp for Vise

All-Metal Bobbin

Flat Nosed Pliers

Half-Hitch Tools

Whip Finisher

Hackle Pliers

Dubbing Twister

Hackle Gauge

Bodkin

Wing Burners

Scissors

Tools

Brian Rose Photo

Pliers

Small-jawed flat-nose pliers make barb smashing easy. Any pliers of this description will work; fly shops often carry them.

Bodkin

Essentially a needle mounted into a post. They are handy, but a hatpin will substitute.

Blender

Useful for blending various types and colors of dubbing. A household liquid blender will work—dig out the wet fur, press it between paper towels, and let it air dry—but the easiest is a dry blender; fly shops carry them. All blenders tend to chop fur, which is either an advantage or disadvantage depending on your needs or preferences. In most cases this chopping will probably be of no consequence.

You can also blend various dubbings by bunching them together, pulling the resulting bunch in half, combining the halves, pulling and combining repeatedly until the dubbings are adequately blended. Hand blending is faster than it sounds, but never as quick and thorough as a blender.

Dubbing Twister

This is used for twisting dubbing in a thread loop. A dubbing twister is occasionally very useful for tying nymphs. A half-straightened paper clip is a fair substitute.

Old Scissors

You can cut hard materials—wire, lead, and the like—with the insides of good scissors (never use the tips to cut hard materials), but with worn or old scissors there is no danger in cutting hard materials with the tips—they're already shot.

Material Holder

Usually either a spring or a clip. It holds long materials out of the tier's way. I'm sold on material holders. As my friend Gordon Nash points out, the spring holder allows you to remove materials from it in any order, which the clip does not.

Whip Finisher

A tool that helps the tier execute a whip finish. I prefer using my fingers, but I know tiers who like and use whip finishers.

Half Hitch Tool

As with the whip finisher, I use my fingers for this work. But some of my friends like and use half-hitch tools.

Wing Burner

These allow you to burn feathers to wing and wing-case shapes. They are handy and fun to play with, but not required.

Bobbin Threader

I no longer use one. If I can't suck a thread end out a bobbin's tube, I'll insert a loop of nylon leader. Besides, there are rumors that a metal-loop threader can scratch a bobbin's tube, and *that* can fray thread.

Hair Packer

Because spun deer hair is used much more often for dry flies and bass bugs than for nymphs and because tightly packed hair is buoyant, nymph tiers have little use for hair packers. But with all the new imitations of near-surface partially hatched insects, we will probably be seeing more nymph-type patterns of spun and tightly packed hair.

If you get a packer, be certain that yours has a small hole—a large-hole packer compresses poorly. I still don't use a hair packer, but some good tiers do.

Hair Stacker

Though only of occasional use in tying nymphs, a hair stacker is a standard tying tool, and it *can* be of value to the nymph tier. A wide stacker will stack a little hair or a lot; a slim stacker will stack only a small bunch of hair, so I prefer a wide stacker. Besides, it is the separation of the hairs that makes stacking efficient, and a wide stacker allows the hairs to really separate. For my own tying, a hair stacker is a requirement.

Hackle Gauge

Like hackle pliers, the main use for a hackle gauge is for dry flies, but I find myself using a hackle gauge frequently for nymphs. Because nymphs may require hackle sizes that don't correspond to the size recommendations on a gauge, you may have to experiment. Find a hackle that looks just right on your Box Canyon Stone, put that hackle to the gauge, and then see how it compares to hook size. Depending on the hook you are using, you might use a hackle two sizes larger than the gauge advises, or three, or neither—you have to decide what hackle size looks appropriate or will offer the appropriate stiffness or suppleness. With some understanding, a hackle gauge is a most useful tool for the nymph tier.

XII

NYMPH HOOKS

It used to be so simple—your pattern listed a hook called a Mustad 9671 so you used a Mustad 9671. There wasn't much else to do—only Mustad and Partridge made fly hooks in any real quantity, and it was common practice to tie trout flies on Mustad, and Atlantic salmon and steelhead flies on Partridge. So most fly tiers paid little attention to hooks, beyond model numbers.

Model numbers alone won't get you far these days. Indeed, the Mustad 9671 is a fine nymph hook, but so is the Tiemco 5262, the Daiichi 1710, and the Partridge H1A, and these are only three of many fly hooks essentially interchangeable with the Mustad 9671. Even though these hooks have much in common, a glance tells that their model numbers have little. To make sense out of hooks today, you need more than just manufacturers and model numbers; you need to understand some basic hook terminology.

There are really only three critical factors in hook selection—-wire thickness, shank length, and size. There are lesser considerations and, as you will see, these are largely subjective.

Wire Thickness

The letter x is somehow firmly connected with fly fishing, especially fly tying. Most things associated with that letter are either mysterious, dangerous, or risque'. There are plenty of opinions regarding which of these adjectives describe fly tying—experienced tiers would choose the first, beginners the first and second, and *very* experienced tiers the third.

An x is used to describe wire that is heavier or lighter than "standard wire," a middleweight wire that serves as a reference point: Standard wire is sometimes called "regular wire." Most nymphs are tied on "heavy wire" hooks, a general term meaning a wire heavier than standard. More precisely, a size-10 "2X heavy" hook has wire two increments thicker than standard size-10 hook-wire. A size-8, 1X *light* hook would have wire one increment *lighter* than standard wire.

Shank Length

A hook's "shank," that usually straight section of hook that stretches from the bend to the tight coil called the "eye," is measured by x's, much as wire thickness is. A "standard length" or "regular length" shank is the norm. A "2X long" shank is two increments longer than standard length. By now, you can probably guess what shank length a size-10, 1X *short* hook will have

(it will be one increment shorter than standard length, just so you can confirm your guess). Shank length usually runs from 3X short to 8X long, even shorter and longer at the extremes. Shank length refers only to the shank—the bend and eye are determined by hook size.

Hook Size

Simple: the larger the number, the smaller the fly. A size-14 hook is about average for trout flies, and a size-22 is tiny. A size-4 is a big trout hook. After size-1, the rules change—now a "/0" tags each number, and as the hooks get larger, the number gets larger too. So a 6/0 hook is considerably larger than a 2/0. Hook sizes are almost always even numbers.

Inconsistencies

Ever wonder why a "large" shirt fits you most of the time, but a "medium" shirt fits you some of the time? It's the same reason why two size-14, 2X long, 2X heavy hooks from two different manufacturers may look different, at least in terms of size, length, and wire thickness—the standards for hooks are not firmly set. They are, in fact, played loosely. The manufacturers keep an eye on each others efforts, but that seems to be the extent of it. So one manufacturer's 2X long may be close to another's

1X long, and such inconsistencies also carry over into wire thickness and hook size. That's why I used the term "increments" to describe shank length and wire thickness. The old rule is that x's actually refer to other hook sizes—a 1X heavy hook is supposed to have the same wire as a hook one size larger and so on—but there is general disagreement as to just how that works, and with no firm standards it wouldn't mean much anyway.

Actually, it's not so bad—even if two 3X heavy, 4X long, size-8 hooks from two different manufacturers are not quite the same length or thickness, either will probably do the same job perfectly well. Besides, with just a bit of experience, a glance at a hook or its picture will tell you all you need to know.

Other Considerations

Other hook considerations include eye angle and bend. Eye's first.

The hook's eye may tip down, a "down eye"; up, an "up eye"; or it may be straight, a "ring eye." Down eyes are the norm for trout flies, but most experienced tiers make this a personal choice.

The three most-popular hook-bend shapes seem to be the Limerick, Perfect, and Sproat, and there are alternate names for these. As you can see by the illustration, they vary little. Each style has its following, but all are time-proven and work. If you haven't already, you will develop your own hook-bend preferences.

There are yet other variations in hook design, and each has its own name. There are variations in barb design, eye shape, finish, and more. But these are minor points, confusing to the beginner and already resolved by the seasoned tier.

More Inconsistencies

Now you know the terminology; the problem is that some of the manufacturers don't know it, or don't use it. A fly pattern may call for a 4X long hook, but the hook you have says "bucktail-streamer" instead of a length in x's. No problem—a bucktail is a long-bodied fly, so the hook you have is probably fine. A glance at your hook next to a picture of a 4X long hook should settle this.

Watch for abbreviations: 2x long may become "2XL", up eye may become "TUE" (turned up eye), and so on.

Then there are the odd hooks, the ones that don't quite fit in. For example, how do you measure the shank length on those nearly round hooks made for caddis-larva and scud imitations?—these hooks have no clear distinction between shank and bend. "English Bait," "Draper Flat Bodied Nymph," and "Stinger"are just a few of the useful, odd hooks available.

The one that bothers me is the "wide gape" hook. If the gape becomes larger in relation to the shank length, wouldn't it make more sense to focus, as usual, on the shank and use a description such as "1X short"? Following this wide-gape principle, a 4X long hook would become a "very small gape" hook. Messy, and unnecessary because we already have a system for this. Perhaps it's our fault. Perhaps tiers pass up a perfectly useful nymph or dry-fly hook because the word "short" makes a hook sound stubby, impractical. Whatever the reason, it bothers me.

The Bottom Line

The trick to understanding hooks is to get a feel for the terms and principles, and then avoid taking it all too seriously. If your thinking runs something like this you'll be fine:

The pattern calls for a "2X heavy, standard length, size-10" hook. My closest hook is described as "heavy wire, size-10." Since the length isn't mentioned, it must be standard. Let's see, my hook looks about like the one in the picture—I'll use it.

I may have been a bit one-sided in all this, focusing on hook manufacturers' shortcomings and overlooking all the good they do. If that's the case, let me set things right. There are far more fly hooks out now than when I started tying, and many of these are imaginative new designs of exceptional quality. We fly tiers owe a considerable debt to hook makers.

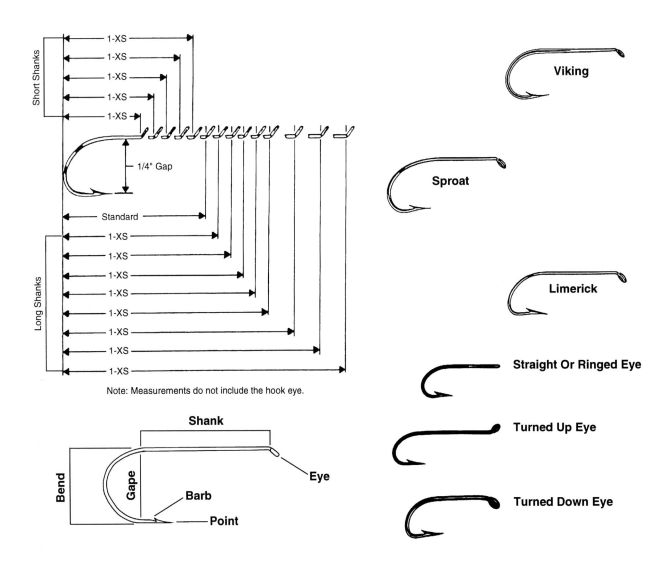

Note: Measurements do not include the hook eye.

XIII

LEARNING FROM THE PROFESSIONAL TIER

A cozy winter evening at the fly vise while the streams are swollen and colored and crusted with ice is the time for unhurried, casual tying; a few stolen minutes of tying much-needed Box Canyon Stones during a brief break in the action during the spring stonefly-nymph migration is the time for tying that is fast and efficient. If you fish the flies you tie, as nearly all fly tiers do, you will sometimes need to tie them quickly.

Though I spend much of my time teaching fly tying, tying flies for display, and writing articles and books on the subject—and have even tied a few hundred dozen flies commercially in the past—I don't think of myself as a true professional fly tier, at least not a production tier. In my experience, a true production tier moves with great efficiency, an absolute economy of motion, to rapidly and gracefully produce fine flies. I don't fit this image, but I've learned a lot from tiers who do. So I now share with you the best of what they've taught me, a bit that I figured out on my own, and even some from a teacher who never once sat before a fly vise.

My friend Doug Canfield, who used to tie more steelhead flies in a week than most steelhead anglers tie in several years, used to let me watch him work on occasion. The first thing he said to me concerning production tying was to "never set down your scissors." That was it; there was no elaboration. But I eventually came to realize how much time tiers waste setting down, picking up, and hunting for scissors. Any way you can hold scissors and still work your fingers is fine, and don't hesitate to switch them from hand to hand as needed.

Efficiency is the key to good technique with any skill. The best guitar teacher I ever had taught me to practice scales and arpeggios very slowly, only a few notes at a time, and to look for trouble areas. "Relax" he said. "Use no more movement than is needed, and for God's sake—slow down if there is even a hint of tension." He felt that tension was the antithesis of efficiency; I think he was right. And he had me practice a scale or an arpeggio or a figure over and over because repetition, as any musician discovers, is the key to efficiency. Incidentally, this guitar teacher was a pianist, never played the guitar, just an indication of how universal these principles are.

Let's take my guitar teacher's principles one at a time and apply them to fly tying.

PRACTICE SLOWLY

This is the only way you can possibly work out the details of good technique.

PRACTICE ONLY A FEW NOTES AT A TIME

Strictly, this would mean tying only part of a fly over and over—generally not practical—but you can tie the same fly in the same size over and over. Tie one pattern one session and another the next if you like, but stick to one pattern and size each time.

LOOK FOR TROUBLE AREAS

If the thoraxes of your Red Fox Squirrel Hair Nymphs are too thin, find a way to easily and consistently gauge the amount of thorax dubbing. If the wing cases on your Gold Ribbed Hare's Ears bunch instead of laying down flatly, take some time to experiment, to figure out what is really going on: Are your wing-case sections too thick? Is the problem in the way that you are holding the sections? Is it the tightness of the thread? A little time spent working these things out will be generously repaid later.

USE NO MORE MOVEMENT THAN IS NEEDED

Are you making large orbits with your bobbin when you could keep its tube close to the hook for orbits that are tiny and quick? Could you eliminate the step of trimming the end of tied-in yarn on your Box Canyon Stones by tying in the yarn at its very tip?

FOR GOD'S SAKE—SLOW DOWN IF THERE IS EVEN A HINT OF TENSION

If you feel tension—in your hands, arms, shoulders, anywhere—stop, seek it out and eliminate it, and then resume tying at a tempo that allows you to stay relaxed. Try increasing speed slightly after a while, but start over if tension reappears.

REPETITION

We've covered that.

But there is more to efficiency than just your movements at the vise. Consider how you set out your tools—are they comfortable to reach? Can you find them in the same place every time? Are all these tools necessary? Are vital ones missing? All this applies to materials too.

Time spent working out tying details will be paid back many times over if it is a fly you tie a lot of. Let us say, for example you are tying size-8 Morristones. Tie in the ribbing and yarn but leave them overlong. When it is time to wrap the yarn, do so without cutting it, even though that's a bit awkward. When the yarn is fully wrapped, trim it so there is just enough remaining to hold onto comfortably. Unwind the yarn and draw it back along the vise. Note the point on your vise where the yarn ends—that is exactly the point where you will cut the yarn every time you tie a Morristone of this size. Do the same with the ribbing. The result: minimum waste and no overlong yarn ends in the way or overshort ones that slip from the fingers.

If you have a memory like mine—limited mainly to such essential details as one's name, address, marital status and little more—it is a good idea to keep a notebook. Make a sketch, jot down a few notes—whatever it takes to make the information easy to retrieve later on. You may tie a big enough batch of Prince Nymphs to last the season, in which case it may be a year or more before you tie them again. A quick review of your information will put you back on track. The big question to ask yourself is this: How many things in this pattern can I measure or gauge in order to increase my tying efficiency with it?

Whenever possible, complete the same step for several flies at once. This means coating the heads of many flies in one sitting rather than each as it's completed, smashing the barbs of a session's supply of hooks before you tie, and preparing most materials before tying—strip the stems of partridge feathers for a bunch of soft hackles and set all the snipped herl aside for Zug Bugs—except when materials are easier to handle at their source, such as goose quills, which tend to dodge your grasp if lying loose.

Professional tiers, in my experience, develop their techniques based on these four criteria: Will it save time? Will it make the fly more durable? Will it enhance the fly's appearance? Will it save materials? There is really no order of importance here; the choices come from instinct, experience, maybe even a bit of wisdom. If a technique increases durability but hurts the fly's appearance, should that technique be used? Depends—how much is durability increased, and will anyone really notice the difference in appearance? Decisions.

So it is efficiency that will make your tying pleasant, fluid, and rapid. And though efficiency can't be forced, if you make a suitable place for it by the way you tie, it will eventually come.

XIV

ADDITIONAL NYMPHS

Mayfly Nymphs:

1. ATHERTON DARK
John Atherton

HOOK: Heavy wire, 1X long, sizes 16 to 10.
THREAD: Black 6/0 or 8/0.
WEIGHT: Lead (optional).
TAIL: Furnace hackle fibers.
RIB: Oval gold tinsel.
ABDOMEN: Half-and-half blend of muskrat fur and claret fur dubbed.
WING CASE: Dyed-blue goose-quill section.
THORAX: same as abdomen.
LEGS: Furnace hackle as a beard or splayed beard.

COMMENTS: Like the Atherton Light and Atherton Medium, the Atherton Dark is an all-purpose mayfly-nymph imitation. All three patterns have been around for some time.

2. ATHERTON LIGHT
John Atherton

HOOK: Heavy wire, 1X long, sizes 16 to 10.
THREAD: Yellow 8/0 or 6/0.
WEIGHT: Lead (optional).
TAIL: Barred wood-duck-flank fibers.
RIB: Oval gold tinsel.
ABDOMEN: Cream fur dubbed.
WING CASE: Dyed-gold goose-quill section.
THORAX: Same as abdomen.
LEGS: Gray partridge-flank fibers as a beard or divided beard.

3. ATHERTON MEDIUM
John Atherton

HOOK: Heavy wire, 1X long, sizes 16 to 10.
THREAD: Brown 8/0 or 6/0.
WEIGHT: Lead (optional).
TAIL: Brown partridge-flank fibers.
RIB: Oval gold tinsel.
ABDOMEN: Hare's mask fur.
WING CASE: Dyed-blue goose-quill section.
THORAX: Same as abdomen.
LEGS: Brown partridge-flank fibers as a beard or divided-beard.

4. A.P. BLACK BEAVER
Andre Puyans

HOOK: Heavy wire, 1X long, sizes 16 to 8.
THREAD: Black 8/0 or 6/0.
WEIGHT: Lead (optional).
TAIL: Dark moose-body hair.
RIB: Copper wire.
ABDOMEN: Beaver fur dyed black.
WING CASE: Dark moose-body hair.
THORAX: Beaver fur dyed black.
LEGS: Dark moose-body hair.
HEAD: Beaver dyed black (optional).

COMMENTS: See "The A.P. Beaver" for information on the A.P. series of nymphs.

5. A.P. OLIVE
Andre Puyans

HOOK: Heavy wire, 1x long, sizes 16 to 8.
THREAD: Black 8/0 or 6/0.
WEIGHT: Lead (optional).
TAIL: Mallard flank dyed olive.
RIB: Gold wire.
ABDOMEN: Beaver fur dyed olive.
WING CASE: Mallard flank dyed olive.
THORAX: Beaver fur dyed olive.
LEGS: Mallard flank dyed olive.
HEAD: Beaver fur dyed olive (optional).

6. A.P. PEACOCK AND PHEASANT
Andre Puyans

HOOK: Heavy wire, 1X long, sizes 16 to 8.
THREAD: Black 8/0 or 6/0.
WEIGHT: Lead (optional).
TAIL: Pheasant-tail fibers.
RIB: Copper wire.
ABDOMEN: Peacock herl.
WING CASE: Pheasant-tail fibers.
THORAX: Peacock herl.
LEGS: Pheasant-tail fibers.

7. BROWN DRAKE
Mike Lawson

HOOK: Heavy wire, 3x long, size 10.
THREAD: Brown 8/0 or 6/0.
WEIGHT: Lead (optional).
TAIL: Dark mottled brown hen-saddle or partridge fibers.
RIB: Gold wire.
GILLS: Gray-brown ostrich.
ABDOMEN: Medium tan-brown fur blended with clear Antron.
WING CASE: Mottled turkey quill section.
LEGS: Brown partridge (or hen saddle) palmered over thorax.
THORAX: Medium tan-brown fur mixed with clear Antron.

8. CATE'S TURKEY
Jerry Cate

HOOK: Light to heavy wire, regular shank, 1X, or 2X long, sizes 18 to 14.
THREAD: Black 6/0 or 8/0.
TAIL: Mallard dyed to wood-duck color.
RIB: Gold wire wound through both body and head.
BODY: A section from a mottled brown turkey quill.
HEAD: Peacock herl.
LEGS: Mallard dyed to wood-duck color tied in as a beard at the thread head.

COMMENTS: Probably a mayfly nymph imitation, but perhaps not. It was originally used in lakes, but it is now used everywhere.

9. FEATHER DUSTER

HOOK: Heavy wire, 3X long, sizes 16 to 10.
THREAD: Brown or olive 8/0 or 6/0.
WEIGHT: Lead overwrapped with wool yarn.
TAIL: For hook sizes 14 and smaller, partridge fibers; for hook sizes 12 and larger, pheasant-tail fibers.
RIB: Fine copper wire, through abdomen and thorax.
ABDOMEN: Natural ostrich herl.
WING CASE: For hook size 14 and smaller, partridge fibers; for hook sizes 12 and larger, pheasant-tail fibers.
THORAX: The same herl used to form the abdomen.
LEGS: The tips of the wing-case fibers.

COMMENTS: Popular, effective. The wing case and legs are handled in the same fashion here as they are for the Pheasant Tail (nymph).

10. FLASHBACK PHEASANT TAIL

HOOK: Heavy wire, regular shank or 1X long, sizes 20 to 10.
THREAD: Brown 8/0 or 6/0.
TAIL: Pheasant-tail fibers.
RIB: Fine copper wire.
BACK and: Flashabou strands.
WING-CASE TOP
ABDOMEN: Pheasant-tail fibers.
WING CASE and LEGS:
THORAX: Peacock herl.

COMMENTS: The Flashabou is pulled forward over the abdomen, secured at midshank with thread turns; then the Flashabou is doubled back and secured with more thread turns, the wing case-leg fibers are tied in, the herl is wrapped over the thorax, and then the rib is wound over both the abdomen and thorax. Complete the wing case and legs as usual, and then pull the Flashabou forward, atop the pheasant, and secure it with thread turns.
  Flashback nymphs are new and hot right now. Time will tell.

11. FLOATING NYMPH
Rene' Harrop

HOOK: Standard dry fly, sizes 20 to 12.
THREAD: 6/0 or 8/0 of a color to match the body.
TAIL: Dry-fly hackle fibers, split.
RIB: Floss of a color to match the natural.
BODY: Antron dubbing to match the natural.
WING CASE: A ball of dark gray poly dubbing spun onto the thread, then slid to the nymph in a clump. The thread is then secured leaving a ball of poly dubbing as a bulging, splitting wing case.
LEGS: Dry-fly hackle fibers tied to each side of the thorax; color should match the natural.
HEAD: Antron dubbing to match the body.

COMMENTS: The floating nymph is presented as its name suggests. Fished dead drift, it suggests a mayfly nymph shedding its shuck at the surface.

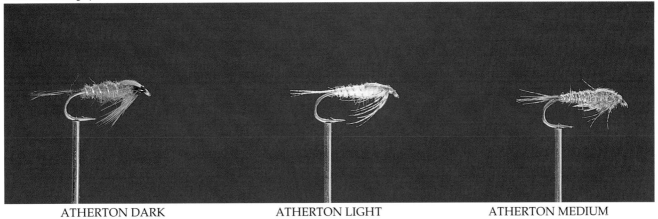

ATHERTON DARK   ATHERTON LIGHT   ATHERTON MEDIUM

A.P. BLACK BEAVER   A.P. OLIVE   A.P. PEACOCK AND PHEASANT

BROWN DRAKE   CATE'S TURKEY   FEATHER DUSTER

FLASHBACK PHEASANT TAIL   FLOATING NYMPH

12. GENIE MAY
Charles Brooks

HOOK: Heavy wire, 2X long size 8 to 3X long size 6.
THREAD: Brown or black 8/0, 6/0, or 3/0.
TAIL: Hackle fibers, grizzly dyed dark orange.
RIB: A thin strand of purple yarn spun with a gray ostrich herl.
BODY: Mottled brown fur or yarn.
HACKLE: Grizzly dyed dark orange palmered up the front half of the body in two turns.
HEAD: The same as the body.

COMMENTS: Charles Brooks's imitation of the giant mayfly nymph *Hexagenia*. Brooks varied the Genie May's materials from book to book and, for me, his instructions fail to produce a fly like those shown in his books. What you see here is my best shot.

13. HEXAGENIA WIGGLE NYMPH
Doug Swisher and Carl Richards

HOOK: Two hooks; one for the abdomenal half and one for the thoracic. The abdominal hook can be any with a ring eye; the thoracic hook should be heavy wire, regular shank, sizes 6 to 2.
THREAD: Olive 8/0, 6/0, or 3/0.
TAIL: Wood-duck flank fibers.
RIB: Copper or gold wire.
ABDOMEN: Light-tan fur, dubbed.
WING CASE: Mottled brown turkey seection.
THORAX: Light-tan fur, dubbed.
LEGS: Wood-duck or partridge fibers as beard.

COMMENTS: The abdominal section is tied on the ring-eye hook, then the bend is sheared off. A loop of leader is slipped through the ring eye, and the leader loop is secured at the bend of the thoracic hook. A bit more dubbing, the wing-case section is tied in, and the nymph is completed as usual. The idea is that the eye-leader hinge gives the nymph life like action. Real *Hexaginia* nymphs range from 1/2 to 1 1/2 inches in length.

14. SKIP NYMPH
Skip Morris

HOOK: Heavy wire, standard length, 1X, or 2X long, sizes 20 to 8.
THREAD: Brown 8/0.
RIB and WEIGHT: Copper wire.
ABDOMEN: Natural hare's mask.
BACK, TAIL, and: Natural pheasant-tail fibers.
WING CASE
THORAX: Natural hare's mask.

Caddis Larvae and Pupae

1. BREADCRUST

HOOK: Heavy wire, regular length or 1X long, sizes 18 to 8.
THREAD: Black 8/0 or 6/0.
RIB: Stripped stem from a brown rooster hackle.
BODY: Orange seal's fur or substitute, dubbed.
HACKLE: Grizzly.

2. DEEP SPARKLE PUPA
Gary LaFontaine

HOOK: Light wire, standard length, 20 to 12.
THREAD: 8/0 or 6/0 of a color to match body.
WEIGHT: One slightly open layer of lead.
VEIL: Antron yarn, combed, tied in at the bend, and drawn forward around the body in a bubble; the color is usually similar to the body color.
BODY: One-half fur dubbing and one half antron dubbing blended and dubbed; the color should match the natural.
WING: A bunch of soft hackle fibers on each side of body; color should match the natural.
HEAD: Marabou strands spun around the thread, or use dubbing.

COMMENTS: This version of the Emergent Sparkle Pupa is made to be fished well down.

3. GREEN CADDIS LARVAE
Dave McNeese

HOOK: Heavy wire, 1X long, sizes 16 to 8.
THREAD: Olive or tan 8/0 or 6/0.
RIB: Fine silver wire.
ABDOMEN: Bright-green rabbit twisted with three to six strands of olive Krystal Flash.
THORAX: Dark hare's mask.
LEGS: Dark partridge-flank fibers.

4. GREEN ROCKWORM
Polly Rosborough

HOOK: Heavy wire, 1X long, size 8.
THREAD: Black 8/0 or 6/0.
WEIGHT: Lead (optional).
BODY: Insect green synthetic yarn.
LEGS: Speckled guinea hen dyed green.
HEAD: Black ostrich herl.

5. GILL-RIBBED LARVA
Larry Solomon

HOOK: Heavy wire, 1x or 2x long (Larry prefers a humped shank), sizes 20 to 14.
THREAD: Black 8/0 or 6/0.
RIB: Fine copper wire.
RIB: A single peacock herl.
ABDOMEN: Green floss.
THORAX: Peacock herl, short.

COMMENTS: The herl rib is wrapped opposite the usual direction; then the wire rib is wrapped in the usual direction to reinforce the herl.

6. LATEX LARVA
Raleigh Boaze Jr.

HOOK: Heavy wire, English bait hook, sizes 14 to 8.
THREAD: Black 8/0 or 6/0.
FOUNDATION: Light-yellow yarn.
ABDOMEN: A latex strip wound up most of the yarn-wrapped shank. the turns of latex should overlap to suggest segmentation.
THORAX: Muskrat, short.

COMMENTS: Latex comes in cream and light tan, many tiers add different colors to latex with marking pens; adding lead is another option.

7. OCTOBER CADDIS NYMPH
Paul Wolflick

HOOK: Heavy wire, 3X long (Paul prefers a slightly humped shank), size 8.
THREAD: Black 8/0, 6/0, or 3/0.
WEIGHT: Lead wire.
RIB: Narrow pale-orange Swannundaze #85.
ABDOMEN: Rusty orange Hairline Dubbin' #17.
HACKLE: One furnace hen hackle.
HEAD: Peacock herl.

COMMENTS: Paul designes his flies to suit the trout waters around his home in central Oregon. The Orange Caddis Nymph imitates the pupa of the fall caddis, a huge orange caddisfly.

8. PEEKING CADDIS
George Anderson

HOOK: Heavy wire,1X or 2x long, sizes 18 to 12.
THREAD: Black 8/0, 6/0, or 3/0.
RIB: Fine gold wire.
ABDOMEN: Hare's mask, dubbed.
THORAX: Pale yellow or olive fur, dubbed.
LEGS: Brown partridge-flank fibers.
HEAD: Black ostrich.

COMMENTS: The Peeking Caddis can be tied weighted or unweighted.It imitates a cased caddis.

9. RANDALL'S CADDIS
Randall Kaufmann

HOOK: Heavy wire, 3X long (Randall prefers a slightly humped shank), sizes 18 to 10.
THREAD: Black 8/0 or 6/0.
WEIGHT: Lead (optional).
RIB: Copper wire.
ABDOMEN: Twisted yarn of any caddis color.
THORAX: Black fur, dubbed; short.

10. RICK'S RAGING RHYACOPHILA
Rick Hafele

HOOK: Heavy wire, 1X or 2X long, sizes 16 to 12.
THREAD: Brown 8/0 or 6/0.
WEIGHT: Lead wire.
ABDOMEN: Bright-green flashy synthetic strands such as Krystal Flash or Krystal Hair, several strands twisted and wound up the lead.
THORAX: Natural hare's mask fur, dubbed.

COMMENTS: Lead is optional. This is Rick Hafele's imitation of the ubiquitous *Rhyacophila*. The brilliant abdomen of this fly suggests the almost glowing green of the larva.

11. STRAWMAN
Paul Young

HOOK: Heavy wire, 2X long, sizes 14 to 10.
THREAD: Brown 8/0 or 6/0.
TAIL: Mallard-flank fibers.
RIB: Pale yellow thread or floss through the spun hair.
BODY: Natural gray-brown deer hair, spun and shaped, not too dense.
HACKLE: Partridge or grizzly hen.

COMMENTS: An early imitation of a cased caddis, the Strawman still has a loyal following.

Stonefly Nymphs

1. BIRD'S STONEFLY NYMPH
Cal Bird

HOOK: Heavy wire, 3X long, sizes 10 to 4.
THREAD: Orange 8/0, 6/0, or 3/0.
WEIGHT: Lead wire (optional).
TAIL: Brown goose biots.
RIB: Orange thread or floss.
ABDOMEN: Brown muskrat or substitute, dubbed.
WING CASE: Turkey quill section.
HACKLE: Furnace or brown palmered over the thorax.
THORAX: Peacock herl.

COMMENTS: A time-tested imitation of the salmon-fly nymph.

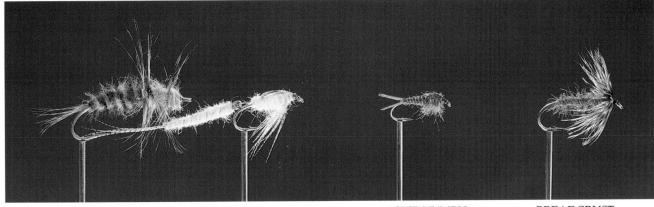

GENIE MAY   HEXAGINIA WIGGLE NYMPH   SKIP NYMPH   BREADCRUST

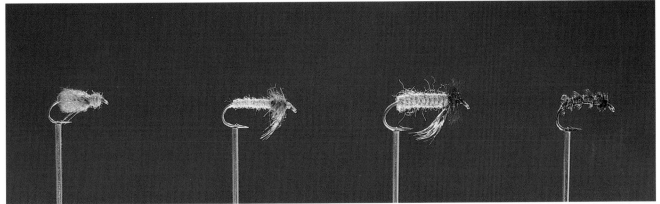

DEEP SPARKLE PUPA   GREENCADDIS LARVAE   GREEN ROCKWORM   GILL-RIBBED LARVA

LATEX LARVA   OCTOBER CADDIS NYMPH   PEEKING CADDIS   RANDALL'S CADDIS

RICK'S RAGING RHYACOPHILIA   STRAWMAN   BIRD'S STONEFLY NYMPH

2. BITCH CREEK

HOOK: Heavy wire, 3X long, sizes 10 to 4.
THREAD: Black 8/0, 6/0, or 3/0.
WEIGHT: Lead wire (optional).
TAIL: White rubber strands.
ABDOMEN: Black chenile and orange chenille woven to put black on top and orange beneath.
HACKLE: Brown, palmered over the thorax.
THORAX: Black chenille.
ANTENNAE: White rubber strands.

3. EARLY BLACK STONEFLY NYMPH

HOOK: Heavy wire, 2X or 3X long, sizes 16 to 10.
THREAD: Black 8/0 or 6/0.
WEIGHT: Lead wire (optional).
TAIL: Dark-gray goose biots.
ABDOMEN: Dark-gray to black fur, dubbed.
WING CASE: Black goose quill section, folded twice.
THORAX: Dark-gray to black fur, dubbed.
LEGS: Dark-gray to black hen-hackle fibers, divided beard style.

COMMENTS: The Early Black Stonefly Nymph is cousin to the Early Brown Stonefly Nymph; see the section on the latter for tying instructions.

4 GOLDEN STONE
Polly Rosborough

HOOK: Heavy wire, 3X long, sizes 6 and 4.
THREAD: Gold 8/0, 6/0, or 3/0.
WEIGHT: Lead wire (optional).
TAIL: Two small bunches of dyed-gold barred teal-flank fibers.
RIB: Thick antique-gold thread (or substitute).
BODY: Gold yarn.
BACK: Dyed-dark-gold barred teal-flank fibers.
LEGS: Dyed-dark-gold teal-flank fibers as a beard.
WING CASE: Dyed-dark-gold teal fibers tied in at the head and extending back over one-third of the body.

COMMENTS: A lot of materials in unusual colors here; it may pay to substitute.

5. GOLDEN STONE
Al Troth

HOOK: Heavy wire, 3X long, sizes 10 and 8.
THREAD: Yellow 8/0, 6/0, or 3/0.
WEIGHT: Lead wire (optional).
TAIL: Goose or turkey biots dyed gold.
RIB: Stripes drawn across the back with a black marking pen.
BODY: A blend of amber, yellow, and gold angora goat and tan fox, dubbed.
LEGS: Dyed-gold partridge-flank fibers, splayed beard style.
WING CASE: Gold-dyed teal- or mallard-flank fibers extending from behind the dubbed head back over one-third of the body.
HEAD: The same fur blend as the body, dubbed.

6. GROVE'S STONE

HOOK: Heavy wire, 4X long (humped or plier bent), sizes 10 to 2.
THREAD: Brown 8/0, 6/0, or 3/0.
WEIGHT: Lead wire under thorax.
TAILS: Monofilament dyed brown or colored with a marking pen.
ABDOMEN: Olive-brown wool yarn (or just brown).
UNDER BODY: Tan wool yarn.
RIBBING: Originally, brown-dyed flat monofilament, but Swannundaze, V-rib, or the like would be good.
WING CASE: A loop of olive-brown wool yarn (or just brown).
LEGS: A breast or flank feather, flat, divided into three sections per side, and each section cemented at its tip.
THORAX: Tan wool yarn.
ANTENNAE: Brown-dyed monofilament (see "tails"0.

COMMENTS: Here's one for the realistic-nymph believer. Time tested.

7. HAIR LEG STONEFLY NYMPH
Gary Borger

HOOK: Heavy wire, 3X long, sizes 10 to 2.
THREAD: Black 3/0.
WEIGHT: Lead wire.
TAIL: Black goose biots.
RIB: Flat momfilament.
ABDOMEN: Black dubbing or yarn. picked out for a fuzzy effect.
WING CASES: Turkey-tail section folded into two sections and lacquered.
THORAX and LEGS: Black dubbing in a dub bing loop and black calf tail spun in that same loop.

8. KAUFMANN STONE
Randall Kaufmann

HOOK: Heavy wire, 6X long, sizes 10 to 2.
THREAD: Brown 3/0.
WEIGHT: Lead wire flattened with flat-nose pliers.
ANTENNAE: Dark-brown or black goose biots.
TAIL: Dark-brown or black goose biots.
RIB: Dark-brown Swannundaze.
ABDOMEN: A blend of claret, amber, orange, rust, black, brown, blue, purple, and ginger angora goat, about fifty percent, and the other fifty of dark-brown Hare-tron, dubbed.
WINGCASES: Three notched, lacquered turkey-quill sections.
THORAX: The same dubbing as used for the abdomen, but heavier and rougher.
HEAD: The same dubbing used for the abdomen.

COMMENTS: Randall ties the Kaufmann's Stone in several hues, to match various stonefly nymphs: tan, gold, black, brown.

9. MONTANA NYMPH

HOOK: Heavy wire, 3X long, sizes 12 to 6.
THREAD: Black 8/0, 6/0, or 3/0.
WEIGHT: Lead wire (optional).
TAIL: Black hackle fibers.
ABDOMEN: Black chenille.
WING CASE: Doubled black chenille.
HACKLE: Black hackle palmered over the thorax.
THORAX: Yellow chenille.

10. RUBBER LEGS BROWN STONE
George Anderson

HOOK: Heavy wire, 3X long, sizes 12 to 8.
THREAD: Brown 3/0.
WEIGHT: Lead wire.
TAIL: White rubber strands.
ABDOMEN: Chocolate-brown yarn and tan yarn woven; brown on top, tan below.
LEGS: Two sets of white rubber-strands projecting from the thorax.
THORAX: Hare's mask fur, dubbed.

11. STONE-FLY CREEPER
Art Flick

HOOK: Heavy wire, 1X long, size 8.
THREAD: Primrose 8/0 or 6/0.
WEIGHT: Lead wire under the thorax only.
TAIL: Two pheasant-tail fibers.
ABDOMEN: One or two stripped ginger hackle stems.
THORAX: Amber seal's fur, dubbed.
LEGS: Grouse-flank hackled.
WING CASE AND BACK: Wood-duck feather tied in at head; the thread is then trimmed, restarted at the bend, and then the feather is secured and trimmed at the bend.

COMMENTS: Art Flick's unusual, time-tested imitation of the eastern stonefly *Perla capitata*.

12. TED'S STONE
Ted Trueblood

HOOK: Heavy wire, 3X long, sizes 10 to 6.
THREAD: Black 8/0, 6/0, or 3/0.
WEIGHT: Lead wire (optional).
TAIL: Brown or reddish-brown goose biots.
ABDOMEN: Brown chenille.
WING CASE: Doubled brown chenille.
HACKLE: Brown hackle palmered over the thorax.
THORAX: Orange chenille, some use a larger size here than in the abdomen.

COMMENTS: A proven old-timer from a pioneer.

13. TERRIBLE TROTH
Al Troth

HOOK: Heavy wire, 6X long, sizes 1 to 4.
THREAD: Dark-brown 3/0.
WEIGHT: Lead wire under the thorax.
TAIL: Dark-brown turkey or goose biots, 1/2 inch.
ANTENNAE: Dark-brown turkey or goose biots, 1 inch.
LEGS: Dark brown neck hackle stems with fibers trimmed close, or black rubber strands.
UNDERBODY: Dark-brown 3/16-inch chenille, double wrapped over thorax section.
OVERBODY: A blend of black and brown seal's fur spun in a dubbing loop and ribbed over the abdomen and thorax. Trim the over body closely, top and bottom.

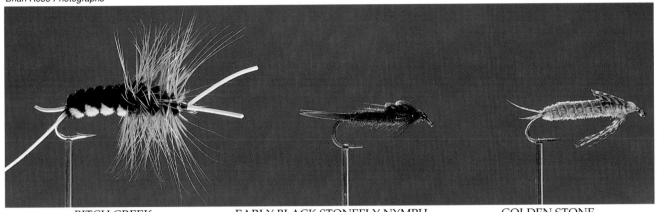

BITCH CREEK   EARLY BLACK STONEFLY NYMPH   GOLDEN STONE

GOLDEN STONE   GROVE'S STONE   HAIR LEG STONEFLY NYMPH

KAUFMANN STONE   MONTANA NYMPH   RUBBER LEGS BROWN STONE

STONE-FLY CREEPER   TED'S STONE   TERRIBLE TROTH

1. ALDER

HOOK: Heavy wire, regular length, sizes 14 to 10.
THREAD: Black 6/0 or 8/0.
BODY: Peacock herl.
HACKLE: Black hen.
WING: Mottled-brown turkey-quill sections.

COMMENTS: This one came from England long ago, and it remains, both there and in America, a popular imitation of the caddislike alder fly.

2. BAETIS SOFT HACKLE
Rick Hafele

HOOK: Heavy wire, 2x long, sizes 20 to 14.
THREAD: Gray 8/0 or 6/0.
TAIL: Blue-dun hen-hackle fibers.
BODY: Gray fur dubbed.
HACKLE: Blue-dun hen hackle.

COMMENTS: To imitate the emerging Baetis mayfly.

3. COWDUNG

HOOK: Heavy wire, standard length, sizes 16 to 10.
THREAD: Black 8/0 or 6/0.
TAG: Flat gold tinsel.
BODY: Olive floss or wool.
HACKLE: Brown hen.
WING: Cinnamon-turkey-quill sections.

COMMENTS: A wet fly from the past with current applications.

4. DARK CAHILL

HOOK: Heavy wire, standard length, sizes 16 to 10.
THREAD: Black 8/0 or 6/0.
TAIL: Wood-duck flank feather.
BODY: Muskrat fur, dubbed.
HACKLE: Brown hen.
WING: Wood-duck flank feather, a single section rolled over the top of the hook.

COMMENTS: Another wet fly from the past with current applications.

5. DIVING CADDIS
Gary LaFontaine

HOOK: Heavy wire, standard length to 2X long, sizes 18 to 12.
THREAD: 8/0 or 6/0 in a color to match the body.
BODY: Blended antron in a color to match the natural, dubbed.
UNDER WING: Soft body-feather fibers extending to the bend; color should match the natural.
WING: Clear (whiteish) antron fibers extending to the bend.
HACKLE: Hen-neck hackle in a color to match the natural.

COMMENTS: The Diving Caddis illustrates one current use for the wet fly: to suggest a female caddis adult diving to deposit her eggs.

6. HARE'S EAR

HOOK: Heavy wire, standard length, sizes 16 to 10.
THREAD: Black 8/0 or 6/0.
TAIL: Brown hackle fibers.
RIB: Gold tinsel.
BODY: Hare's mask, dubbed; make thorax thick, and pick out some of the guard hairs there.
WING: Mallard-quill sections.

COMMENTS: Another useful old-time wet fly, but this one never really went away.

7. LITTLE OLIVE FLYMPH
Dave Hughes

HOOK: Heavy wire, standard length, sizes 18 to 14.
THREAD: Olive 8/0 or 6/0.
HACKLE: Blue-dun hen, four turns.
TAIL: Three or four blue-dun hen-hackle fibers with one turn of thread snugged against their base (after they are tied in) to spread them and tip them slightly up.
RIB: Fine gold tinsel, flat or oval.
BODY: Dubbed—olive rabbit fur in a dubbing loop.

COMMENTS: Dave ties in the hackle first. After the rib is wrapped to just behind the eye, the thread is spiraled back over the front third of the body, the hackle is wound back in two close turns, then spiraled back in two or three more over the front third of the body; then the hackle tip is secured with thread, the thread is spiraled to the eye, and the fly is completed by trimming the hackle's tip and creating a thread head.

8. LIGHT CAHILL

HOOK: Heavy wire, standard length, sizes 16 to 10.
THREAD: Cream 8/0 or 6/0.
TAIL: Wood-duck flank fibers.
BODY: Cream fur, dubbed (usually badger under fur).
HACKLE: Ginger hen.
WING: Wood-duck flank, a single section rolled over the top of the hook.

COMMENTS: Yet another old-time wet fly with current applicatiions.

9. PARTRIDGE AND GREEN

HOOK: Heavy wire or lighter wire, standard length, sizes 16 to 10.
THREAD: Olive 8/0 or 6/0.
ABDOMEN: Green floss.
THORAX: Hare's mask fur, dubbed.
HACKLE: Gray partridge flank (or a substitute).

10. PARTRIDGE AND YELLOW

HOOK: Heavy wire or lighter, regular length, sizes 16 to 10.
THREAD: Yellow 8/0 or 6/0.
ABDOMEN: Yellow floss.
THORAX: Hare's mask fur, dubbed.
HACKLE: Brown or gray partridge flank (or a substitute).

11. PHEASANT TAIL SOFT HACKLE

HOOK: Heavy wire or lighter, regular length, sizes 16 to 10.
THREAD: Brown 8/0 or 6/0.
TAIL: Pheasant-tail fibers.
RIB: Fine gold wire.
BODY: Pheasant-tail fibers.
HACKLE: Brown or gray partridge flank.

1. BAETIS NYMPH
Swisher and Richards

HOOK: Heavy wire, 1X long (I think; this isn't clear to me from their books), sizes 24 to 14.
THREAD: Brown (I think) 8/0 or 6/0.
TAIL: Wood-duck fibers dyed olive.
BODY: Medium-olive and medium-brown rabbit fur, mixed and dubbed.
WING PADS: Black ostrich herl trimmed, projecting back free over the front of the body.
LEGS: Wood-duck fibers dyed olive, as a beard hackle.

COMMENTS: There are a few details on this fly that either Swisher and Richards skipped or I missed, but the essentials are here, and this is a proven, deadly imitation of the tiny Baetis mayfly.

2. BLACK MIDGE
Gary Howells

HOOK: Light wire, 1X short, sizes 20 to 16.
THREAD: Black 8/0.
TAIL: A few black hackle fibers.
ABDOMEN: Dark-brown thread.
HACKLE and THORAX: Plenty of black hackle; trim most of the fibers closely but leave a few intact on each side.

COMMENTS: Often fished awash in the surface. Good in winter streams for the snow-fly midge, and in high lakes.

3. MIDGE PUPA
Marv Taylor

HOOK: Light to regular wire, 3X long, sizes 20 to 12.
THREAD: Black 8/0.
TAIL: Two moose-mane hairs.
ABDOMEN: Floss of appropriate color.
THORAX: Peacock herl.

COMMENTS: The Midge Pupa imitates (obviously) a midge pupa, just about to emerge at the surface.

4. PHEASANT TAIL
Frank Sawyer

HOOK: Heavy wire, regular length or 1X long, sizes 20 and 18.
THREAD: No real thread; instead use fine copper wire.
WEIGHT: A buildup of copper wire at the thorax.
TAIL: Four pheasant-tail fiber tips.
BODY: the butts of the four tail fibers spun around the wire and wound to the eye.
WING CASE: The butts of the four tail-body pheasant-tail fibers.

COMMENTS: After the body is formed, seperate the wire from the fibers and spiral it back to the rear of the thorax. Next, spiral the wire to the eye, pull the fiber butts forward and secure and trim them.

| ALDER | BAETIS SOFT HACKLE | COWDUNG | DARK CAHILL |

| DIVING CADDIS | HARE'S EAR | LITTLE OLIVE FLYMPH | LIGHT CAHILL |

| PARTRIDGE AND GREEN | PARTRIDGE AND YELLOW | PHEASANT TAIL SOFT HACKLE | BAETIS NYMPH |

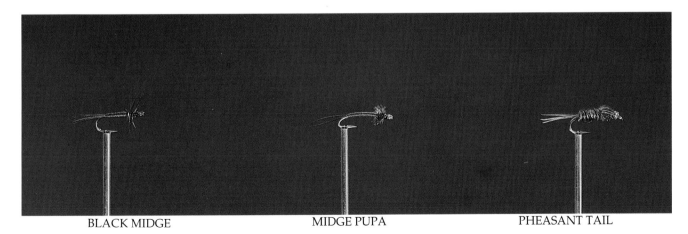

| BLACK MIDGE | MIDGE PUPA | PHEASANT TAIL |

Lake Nymphs

1. ASSOM DRAGON
Charles Brooks

HOOK: Heavy wire, 2X long, sizes 6 and 4.
THREAD: Brown 8/0, 6/0, or 3/0.
BODY: A 1/4 inch strip of natural brown
seal's fur wound in consecutive turns from
the bend to the hackle; other furs, such as
rabbit, are now often substituted.
HACKLE: One grizzly dyed brown, two turns
with the fibers curving forward.

COMMENTS: An odd but productive imitation of a dragonfly nymph.

2. BEAVERPELT
Don E. Earnest

HOOK: Heavy wire, 2X long, sizes 8 to 2.
THREAD: Black or brown 3/0.
TAIL: Pheasant rump fibers (pheasant tail
would be a good substitute), very short.
BODY: Dark beaver fur dubbed heavily.
HACKLE: Black hen hackle, long fiber, sparse.

COMMENTS: A simple but proven dragonfly-
nymph imitation.

3. CANADIAN BROWN LEECH

HOOK: Heavy wire, 4X long, sizes 12 to 8.
THREAD: Black or Red 8/0, 6/0, or 3/0.
BODY: Leech yarn wound and picked or
combed out.

COMMENTS: The original was tied with
Canadian mohair yarn, but today's substitute
is leech yarn. Many other colors than brown
are now used.

4. CAREY SPECIAL
Lloyd A. Day and Tom Carey

HOOK: Heavy wire, 1X long or longer, sizes
12 to 4.
THREAD: Black 8/0, 6/0, or 3/0.
TAIL: Ground-hog hair; a common substitute
is the fibers from a pheasant-rump feather,
but I've seen almost every fiber that will
make a reasonable tail used).
RIB: Black floss reverse wound or gold wire or
copper wire (optional).
BODY: Originally peacock herl, but I've
seen pheasant-rump feather fibers, ground-
hog hairs, chenille, or just about anything.
HACKLE: A pheasant-rump feather.

COMMENTS: This one was incredibly popular in the Seattle area when I first started fly
fishing about thirty-odd years ago. It is a lake
fly originated in Canada that is often suspect-
ed of imitating a dragonfly nymph. I have
seen many variations, especially of the body;
many of which were claimed as the original.
The heart of the Carey Special is its pheasant-
rump hackle.

5. DAVE'S SWIMMING SHRIMP
Dave Whitlock

HOOK: Light to heavy wire, regular shank to
2X long, up or down eye, sizes 18 to 4.
THREAD: Gray, tan, or olive 8/0 or 6/0.
WEIGHT: Lead wire at rear of shank.
ANTENNAE: Tying thread; two to six strands
from 1 to 1 1/2 times the shank's length.
BACK: A strip of clear plastic.
BODY: A blend of sparkle orlon wool, Seal-Ex
(angora goat as a substitute), and beaver belly.
RIB: Gold wire or single-strand floss.
EYES: Leader melted on both ends.
TAIL: A bit of the clear plastic extended from
the back. (Slit or punctured and pulled
down over the eye, I think; this is unclear
from descriptions I've seen.)
LEGS: Picked out body dubbing.

COMMENTS: Notice that this shrimp is
turned backwards on the hook. Shrimps can
swim in either direction, so you can reverse
Dave's Swimming Shrimp on the hook.

6. FLOATING DRAGON
Randall Kaufmann

HOOK: Heavy wire, 4X long, sizes 10 to 4.
THREAD: Olive 8/0, 6/0, or 3/0.
TAIL: Grizzly marabou dyed olive; tie the tail
full but short.
BODY: Olive deer hair, spun and shaped. Color
the back with a brown-olive marking pen.
LEGS: Grizzly marabou dyed olive, heavy at
sides.
WING CASE: A section of mottled turkey with
a notch trimmed at its end. Color the
section with a brown-olive marking pen.
HEAD: Dark-olive Haretron, dubbed.
EYES: Melted monofilament.

COMMENTS: Randall fishes the Floating
Dragon in shallow water on a floating line, or
in deep water on a sinking line.

7. FAIR DAMSEL
Charles Brooks

HOOK: Heavy wire, 3X long, sizes 8 and 6.
THREAD: Brown 8/0 or 6/0.
TAILS: Two dyed-brown grizzly hackle tips.
RIB: Fine oval gold tinsel.
ABDOMEN AND THORAX: Mostly dark-
brown dubbing mixed with some olive,
orange, and black.
HACKLE: Grizzly hackle dyed dark brown
stripped on one side and wound in a few
turns over the thorax.
HEAD: The same dubbing as the body

8. GREEN DAMSEL
Poly Rosborough

HOOK: Heavy wire, 3X long, size 8.
THREAD: Olive 8/0 or 6/0.
TAIL: A short tuft of olive marabou; shear it to
length with your thumb nail.
BODY: Pale-olive fur, rolled into a rope and
twisted tightly around the thread to appear
segmented.
LEGS: Teal, mallard, or guinea body-feather
fibers dyed olive, tied in as a beard.
WING CASE: A tuft of olive marabou.

9. MOSQUITO LARVA

HOOK: Heavy wire, 2X long, size 2 to 14.
THREAD: Black 8/0 or 6/0.
TAIL: Grizzly hackle fibers.
BODY: Stripped peacock herl.
THORAX: Peacock herl.

10. RABBIT LEECH

HOOK: Heavy wire, 3X long, sizes 16 to 8.
THREAD: Black 8/0, 6/0, or 3/0.
BODY: Strip of rabbit hide, with fur, wrapped
up the shank, colors include black, olive,
maroon, and white.

11. SUSPENDER MIDGE

HOOK: Light wire, standard length, sizes 20 to
10.
THREAD: Brown 8/0 or 6/0.
TAIL: A tiny white chunk of foam.
PONTOON: A large white chunk of foam; this
may require doubling the foam. A single
length of foam forms both the tail and
pontoon.
RIB: Fine gold wire.
ABDOMEN: Foam wrapped up the shank and
colored dark brown with a marking pen.
THORAX: Peacock herl.

COMMENTS: The idea is that the pontoon
holds the fly suspended from the surface, like
a real chironomid pupa.

12. SWANUNDAZE MIDGE

HOOK: Heavy wire, 2X long, sizes 18 to 12.
THREAD: Black 8/0 or 6/0.
ABDOMEN: Swannundaze (or a substitute) in
any midge-pupa color.
THORAX: Peacock herl, short.
WHISKERS: White antron fibers tied cross
ways at eye and trimmed closely.

13. TROTH LEECH
Al Troth

HOOK: Heavy wire, 4X long, size 4.
THREAD: Black 8/0, 6/0, or 3/0.
TAIL: Small bunch of dark-brown marabou
fibers.
BODY: Marabou plumes tied in by their tips
and wound up the shank almost as you'd
wrap a hackle. Trim the body top and
bottom; shear off the sides with your
thumb nail if necessary.

14. WHITLOCK CRAYFISH
Dave Whitlock

HOOK: Heavy wire, 4X long, sizes 10 to 4.
THREAD: Brown.
WEIGHT: Lead wire.
EYES: Melted monofilament.
ANTENNAE: Dark moose mane, two hairs..
TAIL: Actually this is the nose; brown deer
hair tips.
PINCHERS: A mottled hen saddle hackle on
top and a cream hen saddle below, glued
together with Dave's Flexament.
HEAD: Brown antron dubbed around the eyes.
HACKLE: Grizzly dyed brown, palmered up
the body.
RIB: Copper wire over the body and back
from the eyes to the tail.
BODY: Brown antron, dubbed and picked out
at sides.
TAIL and BACK: Brown swiss straw or Raffia.

COMMENTS: The hook should be inverted in
your vise. After the body is complete and the
hackle is palmered, the raffia is tied in at the
eye, pulled down, secured with the wire, and
then the wire is ribbed to the eye. Both ends of
the raffia are trimmed. but it is left long at the
hook's eye as a tail. This is another reverse-
tied Whitlock fly.

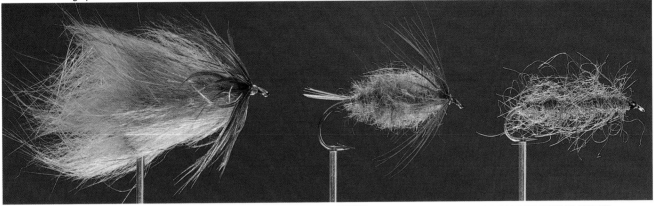

ASSOM DRAGON   BEAVERPELT   CANADIAN BROWN LEECH

CAREY SPECIAL   DAVE'S SWIMMING SHRIMP   FLOATING DRAGON   FAIR DAMSEL

GREEN DAMSEL   MOSQUITO LARVA   RABBIT LEECH   SUSPENDER MIDGE

SWANUNDAZE MIDGE   TROTH LEECH   WHITLOCK CRAYFISH

15. ZEBRA MIDGE
Ken Fujii

HOOK: Heavy wire, 2X long (Ken prefers a humped shank).
THREAD: Black 8/0.
ABDOMEN: One strand of white fly-line backing and one strand of backing dyed or colored with a marking pen. The colored strand can be black, red, or gray; another combination is a yellow strand and a black one.
THORAX: Black dubbing, short and full.

COMMENTS: An ingenious and durable chironomid imitation. Ken fishes it well down in lakes on a very long (up to 25') leader; at the base of the leader, a strike indicator. He lets it fully sink, and then works it back very slowly.

Miscellaneous Nymphs

1. BLACK MARTINEZ
Don Martinez

HOOK: Heavy wire, 2X long, sizes 14 to 8.
THREAD: Black 8/0, 6/0, or 3/0.
WEIGHT: Lead wire (optional).
TAIL: Guinea-flank fibers.
RIB: Fine oval gold tinsel.
ABDOMEN: Black seal fur, dubbed (or a substitute such as angora goat).
WING CASE: Green raffia.
THORAX: Black chenille.
HACKLE: Gray partridge.

COMMENTS: This is a proven old-timer from the Yellowstone area.

2. BLACK WOOLLY WORM

HOOK: Heavy wire, 2X to 3X long, sizes 14 to 2.
THREAD: Black 8/0, 6/0, or 3/0.
WEIGHT: Lead wire (optional).
TAIL: Red hackle fibers.
RIB: A grizzly hackle, palmered.
BODY: Black chenille.

COMMENTS: Once terrifically popular (and still popular), Woolly Worms come in many colors.

3. CASUAL DRESS
Polly Rosborough

HOOK: Heavy wire, 3X long, size 4.
THREAD: Black 8/0, 6/0, or 3/0.
TAIL: Small bunch of muskrat fur with guard hairs.
WEIGHT: Lead wire (optional).
BODY: Muskrat fur, dubbed tightly to creat a segmented effect, then scored to look a bit ragged.
COLLAR: Muskrat fur with guard hairs. The fur is tied in, in bunches around the shank.
HEAD: Black ostrich herl.

4. GRAY NYMPH
Dee Vissing

HOOK: Heavy wire, regular shank or 1X long, sizes 16 to 6.
THREAD: Gray 8/0 or 6/0 (3/0 is optional for the largest sizes).
TAIL: Grizzly hen-hackle fibers.
BODY: Muskrat fur dubbed with the guard hairs left in.
HACKLE: Grizzly hen hackle.

5. HACKLED SKIP NYMPH
Skip Morris

HOOK: Heavy wire, 2X or 3X long, sizes 12 to 6.
THREAD: Brown 8/0, 6/0, or 3/0.
RIB: Fine copper wire.
ABDOMEN and THORAX: Natural hare's mask or any tannish-brown dubbing.
WEIGHT: The copper wire that forms the rib, or lead wire.
TAIL, BACK, and WING CASE: Pheasant-tail fibers.
LEGS: Medium to light-brown mottled hen saddle hackle.

COMMENTS: Tie in the hackle just behind the eye, wrap it *back* over the thorax, secure its tip with the copper wire, and then spiral the rib forward through the hackle in three turns. Could be a mayfly nymph, but this hackled version of the Skip Nymph could suggest a stonefly nymph, especially on a large hook.

6. HACKLED SKIP NYMPH DARK
Skip Morris

HOOK: Heavy wire, 2X or 3X long, sizes 12 to 6.
THREAD: Black 8/0, 6/0, or 3/0.
RIB: Fine copper wire.
ABDOMEN and THORAX: Hare's mask or other dubbing in dark brown.
WEIGHT: The copper wire that forms the rib, or lead wire.
TAIL, BACK, and WING CASE: Pheasant tail dyed dark brown or black.
HACKLE: Black hen saddle.

COMMENTS: See the previous pattern, the Hackled Skip Nymph.

7. KEMP BUG

HOOK: Heavy wire, 2X long, sizes 12 to 8.
THREAD: Black 8/0, 6/0, or 3/0.
TAIL: Three short peacock-herl tips.
BODY: Peacock herl, full at thorax.
WING CASE: Two grizzly hackle tips, flat over front half of body.
HACKLE: Furnace as a beard or collar.

8. LIGHT CREAM BIRD'S NEST
Cal Bird

HOOK: Heavy wire, 1X or 2X long, sizes 16 to 8.
THREAD: Tan 8/0 or 6/0.
WEIGHT: Lead wire (optional).
TAIL: Natural light mallard-flank fibers.
RIB: Fine oval gold tinsel.
ABDOMEN: Cream australian opossum.
HACKLE: Natural light mallard-flank fibers.
THORAX: The same as the abdomen.

9. LINDGREN'S OLIVE
Ira Lindgren

HOOK: Heavy wire, 1x long, sizes 18 to 10.
THREAD: Black 8/0 or 6/0.
WEIGHT: Lead wire (optional).
TAIL: Black hen-hackle fibers.
RIB: Gold wire.
ABDOMEN: Olive marabou fibers.
THORAX: Peacock herl.
LEGS: Black hen hackle wrapped as a wet-fly collar, then trimmed off top and bottom.

10. MATT'S FUR
Matt Lavell

HOOK: Heavy wire, 3X to 6X long, sizes 12 to 6.
THREAD: Brown 8/0, 6/0, or 3/0.
WEIGHT: Lead wire (optional).
TAIL: Fibers from a mallard-flank feather dyed to wood-duck color.
RIB: Oval gold tinsel.
ABDOMEN: Half-and-half otter and cream seal, dubbed.
WING CASE and LEGS: A mallard feather dyed to wood-duck color.
THORAX: The same dubbing mix as used for the abdomen.

11. M R K
Tom Kovich

HOOK: Heavy wire, 2X long, sizes 14 and 12.
THREAD: Olive 8/0 or 6/0.
RIB: Gold wire.
BODY: Olive fur, dubbed.
WING: White poly yarn (or deer hair), short.
HEAD: Peacock herl.

COMMENTS: The MRK may share a common ancestry with the Serendipity.

12. MUSKRAT
Poly Rosborough

HOOK: Heavy wire, 2X or 3X long, sizes 14 to 8.
THREAD: Black 8/0, 6/0, or 3/0.
BODY: Muskrat fur, twisted tightly to suggest segmentation, then scored to appear shaggy.
LEGS: Speckled fibers from a guinea flank feather (or dark teal) tied in as a beard.
HEAD: Black ostrich herl.

13. RUBBER LEGS

HOOK: Heavy wire, 3X or 4X long, sizes 10 to 2.
THREAD: Black 8/0, 6/0, or 3/0.
WEIGHT: Lead wire (optional).
LEGS: Three sets of white rubber strands.
TAIL: White rubber strands.
BODY: Black chenille.
ANTENNAE: White rubber strands (optional).

COMMENTS: See the "Girdle Bug" for tying details.

14. TRUEBLOOD OTTER
Ted Trueblood

HOOK: Heavy wire, regular length or 1X long, sizes 14 to 8.
THREAD: Brown 8/0, 6/0, or 3/0.
WEIGHT: Lead wire (optional).
TAIL: Brown partridge-flank feather fibers.
BODY: Natural otter and cream seal (or angora goat), dubbed.
LEGS: Brown partridge-flank feather fibers.

15. YUK BUG
Al Troth

HOOK: Heavy wire, 4X long, sizes 8 to 2.
THREAD: Black 3/0.
WEIGHT: Lead wire (optional).
LEGS: Three sets of white rubber strands spaced evenly along the shank.
TAIL: Gray squirrel-tail hairs.
RIB: A badger hackle, palmered.
BODY: Black chenille.

ZEBRA MIDGE   BLACK MARTINEZ   BLACK WOOLLY WORM   CASUAL DRESS

GRAY NYMPH   HACKLED SKIP NYMPH   HACKLED SKIP NYMPH DARK   KEMP BUG

LIGHT CREAM BIRD'S NEST   LINDGREN'S OLIVE   MATT'S FUR   M R K

MUSKRAT   RUBBER LEGS   TRUEBLOOD OTTER   YUK BUG

INDEX